ɓ

# NOTHING SO
# CRUDE AS A TIP

Y

*Financial Fables and*
*Cautionary Tales for*
*Stock Market Investors*

Donald Cobbett

MILESTONE PUBLICATIONS

827.914.

# 814748

Published by Milestone Publications
62 Murray Road,
Horndean, Portsmouth, Hants PO8 9JL

ISBN No. 0 903852 26 8

Design Brian Iles
Illustrations by GUS

Printed and bound in Great Britain by
PRINCO (The Netherlands – England – Switzerland)

# Contents

# Foreword by Sir Martin Wilkinson
## Chairman of The Stock Exchange, 1965-73

From time to time The Stock Exchange has been the subject of serious literary examination – attempts at explaining what for so long had been to the uninitiated a dark and mysterious place from which they were excluded. No publicity – no Visitors Gallery and no advertising. There was no knowledge of the lighter side of what went on inside the forbidden building that was visible to the man in the street – only rumours of the indecorous fate of any who managed to evade the guardians of the doors and brave the consequences. Now with this collection of financial fables by Donald Cobbett there is exposed for all to read stories which truly evoke a great deal of humour which to those in the know has always been a considerable feature of life on the 'floor'.

I have known the author for many years and respect both his published work and his talent for putting into words what was needed in many House activities. These fables are not purely and simply humorous excursions, but contours which burlesque so much that is sound practice but yet is also in a sense instructive. They result from a thorough knowledge of his subject, acquired both as a Member and a House representative of the now absorbed Evening News.

I commend this book to all, not least the Members of the Stock Exchange who have grown up in an age that now knows little of some of the subject matter involved, but a great deal about a new world of computers and silicone chips alien to me.

*Martin Wilkinson*

5

# Acknowledgements

Acknowledgement is made to the following for authority to republish in this collection the short stories and financial 'fables' and frivolities named below:

To the proprietors of the Investors Chronicle (embracing the former Stock Exchange Gazette) for – *Millions to Invest, What's in a Name?, Christmas Presents by Computer* (SEG), *The Infallible Tip, I Picked My Broker with a Pin* (SEG), *"Well, what d'you know . . . ?", Fair Shares, It's the Settlement, Developments at Lane End, Dealings on the Kerb, New Brooms, Nothing so Crude as a Tip.*

To the Target Trust Managers Ltd., publishers of the former monthly journal, On Target, for – *Clearing a Path with a Ballpoint.*

To the proprietors of the New Standard (embracing the former London Evening News) for – *The Crystal Ball, Prophet, Dealings Suspended, Never Mind the Figures – What about the Gin?*

To the Syndication Department, The Daily Telegraph, for the following that appeared in the City pages of The Sunday Telegraph – *Losingsore and the Giddy Limit, He who hesitates is lost, Eustace and Amos, Shares that got away, Losingsore and the Three Partners, How can Mr. Losingsore run his broker to ground?, Losingsore and the Forbidden Fruit, The Adrenalin dries up on the Up Line, The Financial Wizard on the 8.12 to Waterloo, Banco on Kropperlabongo.*

To my daughters Judith and Gabrielle
With apologies for your restrained childhood
("Ssch, darlings, Daddy's writing his article!")
and for
Trevor, John and Nick
each of whom will recognize themselves
in parts of this book

# They called me 'The Scribe'
# Donald Cobbett answers his publisher

"What I can't quite reconcile," remarked Nicholas Pine, my publisher, perplexedly, "is how, as a broker-member of The Stock Exchange, you came to adopt the parallel role of financial writer?"

Well, as to that, I can satisfy your curiosity right away. It was like this: with a tentative foot in the market-place, as a humble House clerk, under the precarious conditions of the Great Slump, I had to look around quickly for some means of augmenting the meagre cut of such dealing turns as were gratuitiously put my way as attaché with a small firm of industrial jobbers. It may seem incredible to the present generation of Stock Exchange clerks nurtured on the fruits of inflation, but when I first entered the House market-men pursued all manner of unlikely side-lines far removed from their intended role, to turn the acceptable copper. You could place an order for an excellent walnut cake, get your watch repaired, or buy cheapjack – propelling pencils, scent, razor blades – from a pedlar with capacious pockets.

My own aptitude was for writing, and I turned it logically enough to good account in the specialized field in which I found myself. This was how I came to embark upon my parallel career as a free-lance financial writer for which I was ultimately dignified "The Scribe".

Already by then I had been scribbling hard for several years, my earliest epic being a humorous skit, of which I was inordinately proud, published in the long ago defunct *Passing Show*: my first appearance in the national press, in 1932, a half-century ago this last March. Inspired by this very qualified success, I judged that with my "insider" view-point, and access to a great deal of intimate gossip and pertinent

9

pointers, I might cement some useful contacts among City editors.

At that time, company news was not disseminated with the same dispatch, nor in anything like the detail, it is today; communications were often literally pedestrian; the Stock Exchange itself still shrouded by impenetrable veils of secrecy. Then the financial journalists had to haunt Throgmorton Street for their stories, instead of picking them up, at the touch of a button, through the various piped and relayed channels, or as a result of invitations to prestige luncheons.

By the spring of 1934, convinced, after nine months in the market, that I had acquired all the necessary experience to pronounce on investment matters, I made my first, intrepid appearance in the small, but even then extremely old-established, *Financial World*. This weekly occupied offices among the chimney-stacks of a delightfully ramshackle building (since demolished) in Union Court, off Old Broad Street. It was owned and edited, with the assistance of a charming gentleman named Leighton, by a Mr. Stephens whom I managed to persuade as to the likely value of my services. Somewhat to my surprise, I was quickly designated "Veritas", the pseudonym under which appeared the paper's regular market commentary interwoven with share discussions (tips). So, for the first time, if as it turned out, but briefly, I found myself a financial columnist. It was a role I was subsequently to fill on another half-dozen occasions, not least for the vanished *Statist* (12 years) and the merged *Stock Exchange Gazette*. On the latter, I was given my chance by that doughty Yorkshireman Derrick Boothroyd, who wrote the dryly funny novel, *Value for Money*, all about his native Batley, and subsequently made into a film there with the Rank Organization.

In those days of low cost printing, and no enforced over-manning editorially, it was possible to sustain a small financial weekly on a virtual shoe-string. Nor was mere circulation the criterion of survival: I doubt whether the *Financial World*, at the time of my visitation, had a print order in excess of a thousand copies per issue. What was important was old-establishment and the quality of readership. Many journals so endowed lingered well into the post-war period on an exclusive niche carved in the previous century. *The Statist*, for example, was reputed to have had the backbone of its circulation in club subscriptions. With the *Investors' Guardian*, in its original form, it was the detailed record of company registrations which held a certain following.

The City of which I write was a cosy, intimate place, with convenient wheels within wheels. The faces at the bars were regularly familiar, if steadily aging; everybody, the sweet sellers from their nooks and crannies, the newspaper "boys", the hot chestnut man in winter, Mr. Douch – yes, unbelievably, Mr. Douch, our chemist in Throgmorton Street, who dispensed enormous glasses of fizzy, flowing restoratives for thick heads – knew one another. To the well-established financial weekly, therefore, because it had long been on the lists, accrued what is known as "financial advertising" – mainly the carriage of charimen's annual statements, duly abridged. The mining and rubber secretariates, in particular, acting centrally for a number of the smaller producers, had allocations of money for publicity. This they channelled out, in turn, to the City advertising agents, who took the view that if a journal had always had a modest cut, they would always get it. It was part of the Old Boy's act that ensured small publications enough with which to tick over so long as the proprietor's ambitions ran no higher than a few pints on his way home from the office. Naturally recipients were expected to reciprocate with helpful editorial, and the due puffing of such shares as might need, shall we say, a little "promotion" to the mutual benefit of a nicely rounded circle.

The majority of investors, one finds, has an imprudently earnest respect for the printed word when devoted to matters of investment. It was this gullibility that the "bucket-shops" (nefarious share dealers and pushers run off the scene by the Prevention of Fraud (Investments) Act 1939) exploited through their earlier ability to solicit clients and inquiries by circularizing in receptive quarters. The great bone of contention with members of the London and provincial stock exchanges was that they were debarred by their professionalism from publicly advertising their services, and were at a disadvantage compared with what they contemptuously dismissed as "outside" brokers. Which was not wholly fair, I would add, because some cherished high reputations for impeccable dealings.

For the downright "bucketeer", however, the circular, pamphlet, or sometimes even expensively produced newspaper, was his shop window, and the goods displayed had to appear solid and respectable. Behind the facade there was often little or no substance – just a mailing address. I well remember responding to one advertiser for a financial free-lance, only to find, on arrival, a dusty, one-room office completely bare except for a trestle table, two deal chairs, and a dangling electric bulb.

11

From the lower rungs of the financial writing ladder, I elevated myself by the end of that year – 1934 – to the rarified heights of *The Economist*. In December, I was invited to contribute nothing less than a full-page assessment of the pending Kaffir dividend season. I had already by then ingratiated myself with that journal's deputy-editor, Hargreaves Parkinson, who was kind enough to think well of my efforts, having earlier used several short pieces in his investment section. In his letter of acceptance, he warned me not to be surprised at how it read in print, because it was the practice to regard such articles "merely as material for the views expressed – to fit them, so to speak, into a procrustean bed, from which they emerge in a form which has come to be regarded as characteristic of the paper." I may add that I was then more interested in his concluding assurance that I would be – "remunerated proportionately".

By just dropping in uninvited, I was able then to get on friendly terms with a succession of City editors – Maurice Green, when on the old independent *Financial News*, the kindly Chisholm, of the *Financial Times*, Arthur Kiddy, doyen of his kind, of the immaculate *Morning Post*, also the affable, if earthy, Arthur S. Wade, of the *Evening Standard* just over the "Street" in Warnford Court. Quickly I was contributing bits and pieces to them all, as well as to Holmes, of the *Investors Chronicle* and his often rather testy rival, Henry Dick, of the *Stock Exchange Gazette*. I once saw my offerings in four different titles on the same day. But no "by lines": they appeared anonymously in other people's columns.

On top of this fragmentary writing, plus a new departure for Catholic journalism with a weekly City Column in the *Catholic Herald*, I was asked to do a regular article, "Points of Practice", in a new monthly magazine, the brain-child of a competent writer and publisher, Francis Lewcock. Most of the Stock Exchange's official publications, not least its Daily Official List and Year Book, evolved from private ventures aimed at fulfilling an obvious need. So it was with *The Stockbroker*, launched in 1936, with the tacit goodwill of the Stock Exchange, and aimed deliberately at a House circulation, as it gave coverage of clubs, social and sporting events. For my article here I first used my main pseudonym "Marketeer". After the war, as part of its public relations effort, the Stock Exchange published its own monthly, *The Stock Exchange Journal*, instituted in 1955. Again, for this, I was a regular contributor for many years, and later revised its lay-out.

*A Prefatory Tale: They called me 'The Scribe'*

It was also in connection with the pre-war *Stockbroker* that I first co-operated with my late friend John Kennedy, that most talented of all House artists (and they were many), who signed himself laconically "Jonk". Frequently sketching on the pink blotting pads thoughtfully supplied around the market, in those bygone days of pen-and-ink, and applied to many purposes other than blotting, John preserved with a penetrating insight for character, but always most sympathetically, several generations of Housemen. He once told me how he survived the tedium of scholastic study at Eton by caricaturing everybody in sight, and at an HQ in France, during the Great War, he added what he described as his "nonsenses" in the visitors' book on the opposite page to the signatures. In this way it chanced that he sketched James Barrie. Jonk illustrated my text in *The Stockbroker* with his character studies. And it is his pencil sketch of myself, the very last he did in the House, that heads these reflections.

But my formative years as a writer were post-war. Then I ranged with my contributions as widely as between *The Banker* and *Honey*. Then I met and worked as a free-lancer with many of the latterly famous – Timothy Raison, who in the early '50s, was editing the investment section of the old *News Review*; Don (now Lord) Ryder, who, like myself, then but lately demobilized, was editing the *Stock Exchange Gazette*, for which I wrote a series on Stock Exchange practice. And there was perhaps the greatest of women financial writers, Margot Naylor, who arrived at *The Statist* in 1962 when I was still conducting my weekly commentary.

During the '60s, the late Harold Wincott and I, with totally different styles and approaches, may fairly claim to have pioneered the humorous treatment of economic and investment matters. Under the editorship of John Cobb, I was the first to write pure fiction for the financial press, in the *Investors Chronicle*, and continued to contribute finance in fictional form to that weekly, also to the London *Evening News*, to which latter I sold a week's run of short stories, under the overall caption "Money Maze", in 1968. My object throughout was to bring out, or underline, a valid point of investment practice by burlesquing the subject. This I did effectively for the late Patrick Hutber, in the *Sunday Telegraph*, with my character Mr. Losingsore, the invariably unsuccessful investor, and his compliant stockbroker Angles. Patrick ended his last letter to me . . . "Please keep sending them." These were the purest "financial fables", and this I called them.

13

*Nothing so Crude as a Tip*

I came back from the war to many constraints placed on those having what was officially called "Press Connections". At the turn of the Peace, when share prices were lifting rapidly from their wartime destruction, the Stock Exchange uncovered a mare's nest of manipulation between certain half-commission brokers and outside journalists, the latter engaged in writing up shares to enable their market confederates to unload previous purchases at a profit. The retribution, punishing innocent and guilty alike, was the strait-jacket of Rule 93 (since replaced), which required members and clerks who wrote for, or in any way serviced, the Press, to register such connections, and to seek renewed permission annually to work for clearly specified publications. One of the conditions of such permission was that the contributor should never allow the disclosure of his name or that of his firm. This was "advertising", for years the great taboo in the marketplace. Yet, in practice, this restriction was always regarded imaginatively concerning any House writer of standing.

In 1968 an amusing instance of the elasticity of so many of the official decrees occurred when Authority received a member's complaint that Mr. Cobbett was wantonly "advertising" through the publication of his name. The complainant referred to a brief article of mine on House humour which appeared on the leader page of the *Evening News*. Said the important permanent official before whom I was summoned (we had known each other from youth), "Help me to concoct a reply to this one." I suggested that he should point out that it was a magazine-type article of general interest, and that, as it had nothing to do with investment as such, I had felt justified in contributing it under my own name.

This little incident was directly responsible for my adopting another of my pseudonyms – "Donald Buckley". The *Evening News* was then just about to publish the week's series of short stores on City tycoons, ticker tapes, and booms without end, to which I referred earlier. I explained in dismay, since it was to be a useful boost to my efforts, that the stories were already in print under my own name, and ready for immediate appearance. After some head-scratching among the officials with whom I was closeted, it was agreed as a charming compromise that I should substitute my mother's maiden name – Buckley. But, then, everybody in Throgmorton Street knew perfectly well the identity of Donald Buckley!

Having now explained – or excused? – my emergence as a financial

14

scribe, it remains only to explain, to the particular point of this bedside paperback for the restless investor, that those of my little frivolities and financial fables I have chosen to collect up appeared in the press between the years 1966 and '74. To those who may say "Old hat!", I should emphasize that this span of nine years was probably the most important of any since the discovery of the Witwatersrand in 1886 and the resultant Kaffir Boom which reached its peak of frenzy in 1895. In succession, we had the demolition of the old building, the exodus of the elderly, who had lingered beyond their time to man the House during the Second World War; the explosive entry of the post-war generation, lured to a Throgmorton Street reputedly paved with gold. "It's a licence to kill you need here today," I overheard one youthful cynic remark. While some institutional advertiser in the *Financial Times* blatantly sought a "Financial gun-slinger!"

The new Stock Exchange, with its 26-storey tower block, was rearing up from the descending rubble of the old, and the lady practitioners, headed by my old, friendly adversary, Murial Wood, were knocking impatiently at its hardly opened portals. With all these, and more, challenging diversions, and a vacuum in experience between the old hands and callow youth, we were engulfed by the visitation from Down Under gamblers in the form of their Nickel exploration boom, dawning in 1967 and ending with a calamitous backlash in early '71, when stockbrokers' returns covering unsettled Australian mining share transactions were being called for in continuity by anxious market authorities. Some of my short stories are of pertinent interest, as almost alone among commentators at that time, I persistently derided the Aussie fireworks, and warned, if obliquely, of the obvious perils of over-speculation. Thus, in *The Crystal Ball*, with its *"Fortune's Favourite Gold Areas*, on which nothing had smiled for sixty years . . .''*; and commenting after the event, in December, 1970, in the title tale for this book – *Nothing so crude as a tip*, a prophetic imagining, if ever there was one, in which I visualized the high-flying *Poseidon* (once topping £124 per share) stricken to 30p, and retrieving its fortunes on gold. This, at the time, satirical vision was afterwards proved partially correct, since *Poseidon* took over the old *Lake View and Star*, one of the first gold producers established on the legendry Golden Mile, and resumed the treatment of gold-bearing ore.

In denial of any "Old hat" detractors, I can confidently rely on my friends in the market where our style of humour traditionally dies remarkably hard. For example, there is the instance of the late Horace Ryan, stockbroker, who sometime early between the wars played in a parents' cricket team, in his daughter's schooldays, and unfortunately got out for a duck. For ever afterwards, when he appeared on the "floor", he was greeted with clapping in the approved pavilion style, and supportive cries of "Well run, sir!" In the same way, I feel that market-men will continue to extract enjoyment from my satirically "insider" piece ("Never mind the figures – what about the gin?") concerning the customary wait for a certain major company's result religiously brought to the Stock Exchange by taxi – and always seriously impeded by the morning traffic.

Since human nature basically does not change – which is, after all, the central fact of chartist lore – the vital pointers to wise investment practice I purposely invert with burlesque treatment, as in the "financial fables" I contributed to the *Sunday Telegraph*, are truths for all seasons and every succeeding generation of investors. Indeed, all I have needed to do throughout these pieces has been to update figures – such as salaries, left ludicrously low by the march of inflation – and to convert in some cases from L. s. d. to conform with the February, '71, switch to decimal currency, with the sole exception of the story *New Brooms*, written in December, 1969, and based on the then impending currency change. Although the City Code on Take-overs and Mergers came into force in March, 1968, my many allusions to tips and tipsters, and to insider dealings, were made in times far less restrained than today, partly as a warning against reckless speculation; partly as an admonishment to the background tipster and his too receptive dupe. In *Dealings on the kerb*, Mrs. Fynly-Claver's stockbroker was only too conscious of his client's gross indiscretion doubly compounded by his own.

And, finally, I must sincerely thank Nicholas Pine, my sporting publisher, for putting his foot where others feared to tread; Sir Martin Wilkinson, for forewording my financial 'fables' and frivolities; and the several City Editors and others who have so generously approved my efforts both to amuse and instruct.

May 1982                                                        DONALD COBBETT

# Millions to Invest

George Trivett had spent so much of his time mooning imaginatively about make-believe millions that, by the time he was forty-five, he was still plodding along in the same dreary rut at eight thousand a year with a minor Ministry in Whitehall.

Rags-to-riches tycoons, gold-plated limousines, and the heady flight with the Million-pound Note, always had a fairy tale fascination for George. He fancied himself the threadbare vagrant who picks up a discarded bookmaker's ticket, wins the first elusive hundreds on a sustained objection, and goes on to make a fortune in a lucky dip on the stock market.

He dreamt so much of millionaires that at times the office tea savoured of champagne, his cheapest filter tip seemed the opulent cigar.

At first he ventured unavailingly with competitions. But, try as he might with slogans, crosswords, putting this or that in order of merit, or finding obliterated footballs in pictures of posturing players, not so much as a plastic beaker came his way.

Then he moved to higher planes. He entered a share competition in a popular daily – and won. So did 1,445 other entrants, with the first prize of fabulous thousands dissolving to £3.15!

But this success, modest as it was, opened up a new world in which he could give full rein to his visions of riches. He was properly bitten by the investment bug. Borrowing his boss's *Investors Chronicle* each week, he began ardently to study the theory of investment, experimentally following the course of selected shares and, finally, compiling what he called his "portfolio."

Mrs. Trivett complained volubly over the neighbour's teacups about her husband's lack of enterprise.

"George," she would say tartly, "don't talk to me about George! Spends all his time dreaming over what he calls his investments. Everlastingly figuring away with his bits of paper when he could have been bettering himself. He's never invested in more than a fifty-pence savings stamp in his life."

"He was telling me he made a million pounds the other day," interrupted little Mrs. Crick.

"Million fiddlesticks," corrected Mrs. Trivett. "If he hadn't been woolgathering all the time, we wouldn't have been in Gilbert Villas for the past twenty years."

But George was too engrossed in his pursuit of paper fortunes to heed his wife's scorn. He quickly mastered the scale of expenses, correctly working out his purchases and realizations, and then extended his studies to yields and dividends, scrip and rights issues. Managing his investment accounts gradually absorbed all his spare time.

*"A young man called one afternoon . . ."*

For her part Mrs. Trivett aimlessly played the pools – to the rash extent of thirty pence a week. Not that she had any faith in her luck, but with George endlessly scribbling away in his corner of the parlour, and what with the telly still needing repair, she had to do something. So she mechanically filled in her treble chance with random Xs.

But when George finally lost his second million his wife embarrassingly came up on the treble chance. A charming young man called one afternoon, begging composure, and informed her that she had won £38,673 and some odd pence.

After the formalities of presenting the cheque at the local cinema during which Trivett took a discreet back-seat well out of his wife's limelight, they returned with the pool promoters' representatives to Gilbert Villas. It was then, when they were in the parlour and the British-style port had been dispensed, that the question arose as to what Mrs. Trivett should do with her winnings.

The pools men offered the assistance of their professional advisers, but, much to everybody's surprise, Mrs. Trivett indignantly declined any such assistance.

"Certainly not," she said decisively. "My husband, you know, happens to be an expert in such matters. He has been highly successful with his own investments in the past. I will leave matters to him, thank you very much."

At this totally unexpected acknowledgment of his financial acumen, the surprised Mr. Trivett spilt his port which, in his wife's frenzied search for a dishcloth to wipe his suit, happily diverted attention from her curt refusal of assistance.

Trivett didn't sleep that night. The thought of investing real money filled him with foreboding. What if his wife's thirty-odd thousand went the way of his last imaginary million? In fact, in the subsequent weeks, he was so conscious of the dire domestic consequence of losing even a hundred pounds that he proceeded to invest with a caution that would have made the trustees of the Widows, Orphans and Retired Clergymen's Provident Fund look like West End gamblers.

For their part the pools promoters, suspecting some violently erratic outcome to the stewardship of such a literal backroom boy as Mr. Trivett, took a more than usual interest in his investment policy. Suspiciously, on the pretext of seeking his expert advice, their counsellors revisited him after a year and asked, by the way, how his selection had prospered.

Much to their surprise they found that Trivett had done considerably better than their own panel of stockbrokers. Confining himself to the bluest of blue chips and the primest of prior charges, his wife's portfolio had by then appreciated to £43,000, giving a rather higher income than might have been expected from such securities, due to increased dividends and scrip issues.

Privately impressed by his judgment and flair, the pool promoters took to consulting him from time to time on other clients' investment problems and, finally, on the unfailing accuracy of his advice employed him permanently among their professional advisers.

By this time the Trivetts had moved to a mock-Tudor residence in the Surrey stockbroker belt. Apart from buying his own *Investors Chronicle*, Trivett's study shelves contained every conceivable book on the practice of investment, the mechanics of the market, taxation, accountancy and company law. There were statistical cards, chart services and mechanical calculators readily to hand. He even wrote for the financial Press. In the course of time, with a comfortable capital sum more than sufficient to sustain his wife and himself in their declining years, and with a useful pension from the pools firm, George finally decided to retire. With time on his hands he might finally have succumbed to the urge to display the Midas touch.

Caution imposed over the years in advising on other people's nest-eggs fortunately inhibited this latest urge. Instead, as an entertaining pastime, he reverted to keeping imaginary portfolios. And within a year he had lost a million pounds.

# What's in a Name?

Among the half-a-dozen shrilling 'phones on Monday morning was an irate, and consequently the more inarticulate, Mr. Smith complaining at the absence of his contract note for the purchase (as he evidently supposes) of 1,000 *Ballyhoo Mining*, which have meanwhile jumped twenty-five pence a share and look destined to jump another.

Is it in the confounded post? Mr. Smith queries.

"Which Mr. Smith is that, please?" patiently pleads the Stats Clerk, to whom the call has been put through as a matter of principle because he is conveniently rooted to his desk under a welter of investment schemes, while everyone else is equally conveniently "Out" on the vestibule indicator board.

"J. P. M." roars the 'phone blurring under the impact. "Who the dickens owns J. P. M. Smith?" desperately inquires the Stats Clerk, covering the mouthpiece with his hand. "And for which Smith did we book a purchase of 1,000 *Ballyhoo* on Friday?"

There is a confused rustling around the office as sundry minions bury themselves in fluttering heaps of contract copies and ledger sheets like so many Light Sussex subsiding in farmyard straw.

Some helpful body then unearths the bought butt on which the bargain was originated in the dealers' box, but this turns out to be largely indecipherable, except for the description, number and price of the shares. All these are painfully legible.

The contract copy, in due turn, shows the machine operator to have had a commendable shot at "J. C. M. Smith". This turns out to be one of two clients left behind in the sullied wake of a departed half-com.*

*A broker who receives half the commission his dealings generate.

*Rooted to his desk under a welter of investment schemes*

man, and who nobody technically "owns" at all. The half-com. man's divers problems, of which there are many, still linger around the office propelled on their endless course by memos, requests and entreaties.

But has J. C. M. got the contract note?

Not so, as it emerges. By no means as promptly as J. P. M., some other Smith in the vague lineage, when he has made quite sure whether *Ballyhoo* are up or down, will ring through with profuse thanks at having at last been remembered for a "good thing".

On hurried reference to the card index of clients, this turns out to be the Senior Partner's aunt's cousin, who hasn't dealt since 1965, and certainly isn't entitled to any gratuitous "turns". Unfortunately he is undoubtedly the recipient of the missing contract, albeit his initials are, in fact, J. V. M. A readily excusable typing error, though.

By which time the clerk in charge of the price board has chalked up *Ballyhoo* another fifteen pence to 145p.

This is the last straw for the Stats Clerk, who abdicates. "Better tell the office Partner," he decides in desperation.

Summoned from pre-luncheon refreshment in the boardroom, that gentleman is acquainted with the situation, which he doesn't find conducive to his digestion.

"Right, what we've got to do," he says, eyeing the price board, "is to cover the real buyer's order. Tell the Head Dealer, and charge the loss to Mistake Account."

"What about advising J. V. M. to take his profit?" helpfully suggests the Stats Clerk. "We can do a put-through."

"Good. Ring him up and suggest it."

"What about J. C. M.?" protests the Chief Cashier, a stickler for the niceties. "The bargain has been entered in his account."

"Blast J. C. M.!" explodes the Office Partner, as Ballyhoo are marked up a further five pence.

The dealers' box reports back that the put-through has been done on the basis of 151p–153p.

"Blast again," says the Office Partner, and retreats ginwards. *Ballyhoo* are marked back twenty-five pence, but he has already gone.

# Christmas Presents by Computer

The Management Master hummed to itself in neutral. It was big, shiny, clinically clean, and totally devoid of imagination. It was also extremely expensive. It had cost the firm of stockbrokers, with appropriate programming, upwards of £300,000 to install.

The Senior Partner regarded it now with undisguised suspicion. Its serried rows of the dials stared unblinkingly back at him. He had first joined the firm when elderly clerks in black alpaca jackets, seated at high desks, laboriously inscribed the books in meticulous copperplate.

He had never taken kindly to even the most limited forms of office mechanisation. It was his younger partners, on the thin end of the profits, who had inveigled him further and further into its trammels, and as more and more machines came in members of the staff, whom he had known all his life, were gradually displaced.

Finally came their insistence on full computerization as the only means of surmounting the hurdle of ever-rising office costs. It would enable them, they assured him, to concentrate the firm's entire accounting here in the basement with one skilled operative – clients' and jobbers' accounts, wages, taxation, the lot, even down to the last ha'penny stamp. The Master would voraciously consume interminable facts and figures, store them away, and represent them, in any form, at virtually the touch of a button. Wearily the Senior Partner had agreed.

The Master's pimply custodian coughed inquiringly at the Senior Partner's elbow. It was nearing his time of departure, and he had been about to shut the machine down for the night. He was anxious in case his visitation might mean a capricious desire, at this most inconsiderately late hour, to show an interest in the new toy. His chief had certainly not shown the least interest before.

The Senior Partner, for his part, could not have accounted clearly for his being there at all. Except for lunch at the City Club, he seldom these days left the reality, as he knew it, of his own dignified office with its heavy portraits and brocade hangings.

All that day he had been strangely, inexplicably worried. It was four days before Christmas, and with the festival on a Sunday, business, such as it was, had already dwindled to vanishing point. Most of the staff had already been sent home, he supposed, because on opening his door the outer offices were unaccountably quiet. But then they had been quiet, now he came to think of it, for some time past. Only the uniformed messenger stood guardian in the vestibule.

Poor Bateson, he thought, no Christmas bonus for him this year. None for anybody, so he had been told, for the first time in his memory. The decision had been taken that morning. Perhaps that was what had saddened him. He could remember the years when his father

*The senior partner regarded it now with undisguised suspicion*

25

had distributed pheasants by the brace and a bottle of port to everybody down to the newest office boy. When the offices were decorated with holly and mistletoe, and vibrated with the sound of merriment.

Now there was only himself and Bateson, so far as he could see. And that blasted contrivance in the basement.

Telling the messenger to wait before locking up, he had wandered off abstractedly down the heavily carpeted corridor, finally finding himself, without any conscious purpose, in the basement.

His question, when it came, was derived from his subconscious musings.

"So this is the machine they tell me is the heart of my firm. Is it true, young man, that it knows everything?" he asked.

"Yes, sir, everything of which it is in possession of the data, that is."

"Does it know, for example, my staff?" persisted the Senior Partner.

"You mean, sir – how many, their names, addresses, ages, salaries, P.A.Y.E. codes – things like that? Yes, it knows all that," answered the pimply youth almost enthusiastically, despite the hour. The Old Boy might be getting the idea, he fancied.

"No, more than that, boy! Does it know what they would like best – what would most make them happy?"

"Happy!" echoed the pimply youth incredulously (he would like to have added, "You're joking!"). He looked round despairingly. He would have to be patient.

"It can't compute an average measure of happiness," he explained. "It only knows money. But money makes most people happy," he added brightly.

"A pity," sighed the Senior Partner. "I was hoping I might personally have given you all something you would specially like."

The youth pondered a moment. That was different. He could see the vanished bonus again miraculously within grasp.

"On second thoughts," he suggested, "perhaps we could get the machine to give a computation of individual merit. We could go on from there and get a formula of reward."

"The most worthy, you mean?" asked the Senior Partner.

"Well, hardly worthy. The rate of reward – your presents, I mean – would be calculated strictly on the capacities and needs of the recipients." That sounded promising, he thought. Personally he had always aspired to a senior partnership, and sufficient to ensure an affluent retirement at the age of sixty.

"Very well," agreed the Senior Partner. "Request a capacity rating."

The operator sat down and typed dexterously at the Master's keyboard. Suddenly the computer hummed into higher frequency, the note growing louder and higher still as it searched through its memory store, circuit by circuit for the information it sought. Even as its whine died away, the keyboard chattered back the answer.

The pimply youth studied the answer with evident satisfaction as the paper curled out from the Master's cabinet between his fingers.

"Well?" the Senior Partner inquired.

"Of the five of us," replied the youth eagerly, "I am given the highest capacity rating. Mabel – the telephonist, you know – the lowest. Poor Mabel, she's quite satisfied with 'pop' records and a hair-do."

The Senior Partner's knowledge of Mabel was confined to his frequent failure to get the number he asked for.

"But five of you," he repeated in perplexity – "only five of you!"

"That's right, sir. All that are left since the Master came."

". . . And of these few, how can the computer apportion reward? If I gave five hundred pounds, for example? Ask it that."

The youth typed the question into the Master. It gave its answer promptly, but the youth scratched his head. Again he asked the question.

"Well, what does it reply?" asked the Senior Partner impatiently.

"It replies," said the youth crestfallen, "give the lot to Mabel."

"To Mabel!"

"Don't you see," said the youth dolefully. "It takes so much less to please Mabel than any of the rest of us, so that she produces the greatest return in terms of happiness. That's how the machine sees it. It's logical."

"Oh, I see," said the Senior Partner.

But he didn't, and in the end he gave a hundred to each of them and left it at that.

# The Crystal Ball

The little estate bequeathed to Charlie Priggett by his late uncle George included a thousand shares in a moribund Australian gold mine that stood at the time of probate the year before, at only a few pence.

Indeed, their price was so low, as the solicitor then pointed out, that the expenses of selling would almost have absorbed what they would have fetched. So with legal exactitude in tying loose ends, he transferred the holding into Charlie's name.

When in due course the new share certificate arrived, Charlie heedlessly stuffed it away at the back of the bureau along with last season's bulb catalogues and a handsome brochure optimistically sent him by Cartier.

Six months later, on the strength of nearby nickel discoveries in Western Australia, he suddenly found his inheritance of a few hundred pounds miraculously transformed into three thousand, and frantically fished for the discarded certificate – and also for the Cartier brochure.

He was buying his wife a diamond wristlet as a Christmas present.

This unexpected stroke of good fortune fired Charlie with unbounded enthusiasm for stocks and shares.

With blissful ignorance of the pitfalls awaiting the novice in Throgmorton Street he proceeded to speculate in a succession of resurrected mining shares, and quickly expanded his capital into five thousand. We fellow-commuters on the 8.24 regarded his meteoric success with interest and not a little envy.

Even the vagaries of winter travel were rendered more endurable by absorbing assessment of the market prospects.

The dulcet tones of British Railways' fair apologists at Waterloo, expounding on the subject of frozen points, were lost on us as we tumbled from our ice-bound compartment in heated argument about the merits of *Fortune's Favourite Gold Areas*, on which nothing had smiled for sixty years, least of all its shareholders.

Charlie, now that he had the bit firmly between his teeth, quickly became a dedicated investor. He equipped himself with all the para- phernalia of the business – slide rule, chart services, statistical cards, financial journals – the lot.

He devotedly supported all the companies in which he held shares, which was all right with *Slashprice Stores*, but difficult with *Multipress Machinery*, as there was nowhere convenient in his garden for a road roller.

"Well, all you need now is a crystal ball," declared old Scrimpot jokingly in the carriage one day. Charlie laughed with the rest of us, but I caught a reflective gleam in his eye.

*Amid a welter of shattered coloured balls . . .*

And then, shortly before Christmas, chancing to take a short cut through City back streets, blessed if I didn't find one of those. Of course, it was to be a joke. We would present it to him, handsomely packed and tied with a golden ribbon, before Christmas.

It was a great heap of decorative, silver baubles in a shop window that gave me the idea.

A job-lot in Christmas decorations I imagined for the shop was one of those furtive little places left behind in the tide of concrete blocks where junk mixed freely with cheapjack.

The balls, the kind you hang on a Christmas tree, but quite unusually big and lustrous, were made in Hong Kong, as I saw when I entered the shop.

They were shoddily packed in boxes of half-a-dozen, but a number had overflowed their packing and lay riotously among oriental armour and Edwardian chambers.

One especially big and luminous ball which lay apart from the rest in a corner of the window, took my fancy.

"May I have this one?" I asked the proprietor, picking it out.

"Take what you like," he replied, laconically. "They're all twenty pence."

I paid him, and stuffed the ball into my briefcase. I was vaguely conscious that it was larger and heavier than I fancied in the case of such decorations.

We elaborately packed the ball that evening in the Blue Boar, and returning the following evening ceremoniously presented it to Charlie in the train after an exhaustive argument about *Sumpsands Oil*, in which he had bought a thousand shares only that day.

Charlie played up to our joke with great gusto, making an immense charade of peering into the ball, cupping it between his hands, as he had seen the clairvoyants do on the telly, and distantly contemplating its depths.

"Well?" we all egged him on.

"I see," said Charlie in what he fondly imagined to be the measured intonation of the mystic, "I see . . . Here, dash it, I can't see a thing with the flashing lights of that train." He laughed, then suddenly became absorbed with the ball again. "Just a minute, though, I can see something – I really think I can."

"What can you see?" we urged in unison.

Charlie looked up perplexed. "Well, just for a second, I really thought I did see something – a waste with a cluster of great pylons – no, oil derricks, that's what they were – derricks.

"Come off it," I gibed, "you've been having too many oil shares. *Very* convenient, I must say. Here, let me have a go."

And then, of course, everybody wanted to explore the future.

I must confess, when I took my turn, there was shadowy movement deep beneath the surface of the ball capable of provoking fanciful pictures.

Also, I noticed something that had previously escaped me – that the ball had no projecting eye for hanging it up, as is certainly usual with such decorations. But I kept this to myself.

That would undoubtedly have been the end of our joke had it not been for the extraordinary coincidence of the takeover bid for *Sumpsands Oil* the very next day.

The shares shot up by fifty pence.

After that, Charlie, plead as we would for a little realism, could talk of practically nothing else.

He thought he'd been provided by some miracle, with the means of the Midas touch.

We got the rest of the story at second hand from our wives who got it variously from Charlie's better-half, Katie.

On Christmas Eve she rushed out and brought a whole pile of tinsel, boxes of shiny balls, and the like, and dumped the whole lot in her sudden recollection that the turkey was still at the butcher's, slap on top of Charlie's bureau where he had carefully left his precious crystal ball.

With a great deal more enthusiasm than discretion, the two Priggett children let themselves go after tea with everything that shone, shimmered or dangled on which they could lay their hands. So by the time Charlie returned from the office, he could only duck his head and utter a stunned "Great Heavens!"

The lounge was a riot of colour. The liberally bedecked Christmas tree was up, the ceiling was criss-crossed with festoons, and from every point of possible attachment hung tinsel, paper chains, and coloured balls and stars.

The next thing Charlie uttered apparently was a profound profanity. Katie heard it even from the kitchen.

"Who's touched it?" demanded Charlie heatedly, as he ransacked desperately.

*Nothing so Crude as a Tip*

"What?" asked Katie, in all innocence.

"My . . . (He was going to say "crystal ball", but amended it quickly to "silver"). I put it on top of the bureau last night," he spluttered.

"Oh!" Katie expressed relief. "You mean the decorative ball your friends gave you for a laugh. Really, how ridiculous you are, Charlie! Why, the children must have accidently put it with the other decorations I got them."

Well, from the almighty fuss Charlie created about that wretched ball, as Katie afterwards related to my wife, you would have thought he'd lost the crown jewels.

The household was thrown into turmoil, as he dragged the kitchen steps into the lounge, and began to search frantically – and none too securely – at ceiling-level among the perfusion of decorations in which he became increasingly more entwined.

With womanly logic, Katie calmly surveyed the growing shambles. Finally, and with infuriating irony, she ventured to remark that wasn't it perhaps his blessed ball on the top of the Christmas tree.

And there, indeed, Charlie saw that it was.

He lent forward eagerly to grasp it, and, in his anxiety, lost his balance. The steps shot from under him, Charlie performed a neat somersault, and landed abruptly in the branches of the stricken conifer amid a welter of shattered coloured balls.

Apart from Charlie's sprained ankle which deprived us of his company at the Blue Boar over the festivities, no damage was done that could not be rectified by one of the children nipping out quickly to the *Slashprice Stores* (*Slashprice* of course) – for a new box of coloured balls and baubles.

We don't see so much of Charlie these days. He is still searching diligently among City back streets for a real crystal ball. But so far he has searched in vain.

# The Infallible Tip

When Titcoombe came into his Aunt Matilda's little nestegg, he was able for the first time in his life to indulge a long-cherished urge for what he dignified as "investing". Some people would have bought a car. Titcoombe bought stocks and shares. However all his efforts brought him no reward, and certainly no pleasure. He was always in the stock market dumps.

"*Cumfy Carpets* off again," he would bemoan, and hurry on.

Not that he didn't try. The cynical fact is that he did. He lived for the financial journals, devoured every textbook on Stock Exchange procedure on which he could lay his hands, and drove a succession of rapidly discarded brokers to distraction. Life in the Saloon Bar became a financial debate about which yielded what, earnings cover, scrip issues, and other mysteries. His wife was driven round the bend, not knowing whether the housekeeping hadn't gone down the drain with *International Sausages*. And his son took to nipping down of a morning to take an early look at the *Financial Times*, so as to judge from the balance of pluses and minuses against the parental portfolio what the domestic climate was likely to be.

Well, matters couldn't go on indefinitely like that, we saw, or what with the expenses of continually jumping in and out of the market, and the losses he was cutting having his mind changed for him every few days, Titcoombe would quickly blue his little inheritance. So we decided that what Titcoombe needed was somebody with the concrete, gilt-edged, infallible tip.

It was ironical that just when we found the oracle, Titcoombe should have been away for the day. It was Raddles who hit on the solution. He declared, with a sudden flash of inspiration, that the very man would be Malchett, an accountant's clerk in the City. Malchett, it appeared, would be coming down for a day the very next week to do a quarterly audit of the firm's books. And further, since Malchett would be working late, he would be staying overnight at the Blue Boar. Of Malchett's inside knowledge of the financial jungle, Raddles assured us enthusiastically, there was no doubt. His firm were big City auditors, and naturally its articled clerks knew more than a thing or two, if they cared to tip you the wink.

Well, as I have said, Titcoombe didn't turn up that evening – that is, not until a few minutes to "closing". His unaccountable absence was very disappointing to us, because – no doubt about it – Raddles had not exaggerated his man. Malchett, striped-trousered, wing-collared, with an air of brief-cased authority, positively bristled with business efficiency, and there was no difficulty in bringing him round to stocks and shares. He got us all into a corner and, with many a sidelong glance over his shoulder, and confidential wink, imparted secrets of the company world that would have sent the absent Titcoombe camp-

*Imparted secrets of the company world . . .*

34

ing out on his broker's very doorstep so wild would his enthusiasm have been.

"... and if you really want to make a packet quickly," Malchett was going on impressively, "I can really give you chaps a winner – seeing you're pals of Raddles here."

"You want to get yourselves into *Consolidated Mixers*," Malchett went on. "You know, the food mixer people. Their Better Batter Beater is an absolute winner. They're building a new factory to double the manufacturing capacity. And I'll tell you another thing. There's going to be a bid."

"What are the shares standing at?" asked Raddles.

"That's the beauty of the thing," said Malchett. "They're low-priced – tenpenny shares standing at thirty-five pence. One can get a lot for a little money. And the take-over price will be double that. An absolute certainty, I tell you." He produced copious statistics on *Consolidated Mixers*, the last balance sheet, and so on, from his brief case, and we really got down to serious business. Then Titcoombe rushed in begging the favour of a quick one. We introduced him to Malchett in the skirmish of departure, and when Titcoombe had got the gist of things, he was half mad about missing such a chance.

"You tricky blighters!" he spluttered. "On to a good thing, are you. Come again, what's the name?"

"*Consolidated Mixers*," we all said. "They're going to be taken-over."

"*Consolidated Pictures?*" Even then he hadn't heard in his excitement, scribbling the name on his shirt cuff with a pencil stump which promptly broke.

"No, *Mixers, Mixers!*" we urged in unison, and then "Time" was called again, and, amid attempted explanations, the whole of the Saloon Bar struggled out into the street.

We all got ourselves into *Consolidated Mixers* next day around thirty-five pence, and became students of the financial columns. For a week the shares remained unaltered, but then, rather disappointing, they dropped threepence. This was merely the ebb-and-flow, we consoled ourselves. When they were twenty-three pence, we agreed it was a temporary setback. When they were another five pence down, we caught ourselves giving disconsolate grunts to our neighbours' cherry greetings. Titcoombe however seemed to be in increasingly good form.

Finally he burst in on us one evening in the Saloon Bar, and stood drinks all round before we could protest – double whiskies.

"Well we've done it, chaps," he exploded. "What a tip!"

"Done it!" we echoed, incredulously. "Have we?" *Consolidated Mixers* were down to sixteen pence.

"Don't tell me you don't know?" Titcoombe surveyed us with a puzzled look. "You must have made a nice bit too. I certainly cleaned up. Good old *Consolidated Pictures*."

And there it was, headlined on the financial page – *Consolidated Pictures* had sold its chain of closed-down cinemas, and was winding-up with the prospect of seventy pence a share.

Now Titcoombe has bought a car as well as being an investor.

# Losingsore and the Giddy Limit

Mr. Losingsore invariably resorts to the daily official "markings"* in final judgment on his broker's dealing prowess. Such researches frequently cloud the amiability of the breakfast table.

Mrs. L. is quick to detect the symptoms: her husband flings down his *Financial Times* with an exasperated grunt, to the peril of his coffee cup.

"Something wrong, dear?" she inquires, with consummate indiscretion. She has bitter recollections of the time their holiday in the Bahamas went down the drain with *Tingley's Slipwear*.

"Oh, no, not a thing!" retorts her husband, scathingly. "Only those blasted brokers dealing for me at the bottom again." He jabs pugnaciously at the Pink 'Un. "Got 32p for my *Hemlock Investments*, and the lowest deal shown here is 34. See for yourself."

His wife stops in her efforts to arrest the spread of a coffee stain, and peers helpfully over his shoulder.

"What's that little thing – like a cocktail onion with a stick stuck through it?" she inquires. "Have you looked at the legend?" Mr. L. hasn't, duly does, and sees that this particular hieroglyphic denotes a bargain done on the previous day. Which makes him more angry than

---

* The daily bargain (dealing) prices, now under computerisation, are extracted from the jobbers' dealings, as recorded in *The Stock Exchange Daily Official List*, probably the most costly newspaper in the world: £1.60 per single copy, at the time of writing. The previous day's "markings" were originally published daily in the *Financial Times*, which for technical reasons now confines such information, restricted mainly to equities and convertible stocks, only to the Thursday's business, published in its Saturday issue.

ever. Crunching two indigestion tablets, he seizes his hat, and slams out of the house.

Muttering to himself, "I'll nail him," he turns into Station Approach to collide with Prickett.

"I'm going to 'limit' my broker in future," announces Losingsore, by way of salutation. "Dashed if I'll always buy at the top, and sell out at the bottom."

"Limit!" echoes Prickett, confused with some low-calorie confection. "Very beneficial, I should say."

Losingsore explains laboriously that he means leave orders with his broker for execution at predetermined prices. This principle diverts fellow-commuters with lively debate until the 8.22 hits the buffers at Waterloo. The Colonel finally rasps, "Anyway, I always leave it to my broker-fella . . . better to deal when you can, that's what I say. Why tie the chappie's hands?"

But this pearl of wisdom falls on stony ground, because Losingsore

*Her husband flings down his Financial Times . . .*

is by this time adamant in his resolve to ensure that his broker really exacts the last ha'porth out of the market. Deciding to switch the *Hemlock* proceeds into *Consolidated Twisters*, he phones Angles, his broker. ". . . and don't pay more than 74 pence," he adds, which is well outside what is humanly possible at the time.

After a perspiring sprint round the market, Angles is quickly back reporting apologetically that 76 is definitely the cheapest offer he can find, and the jobbers seem generally short of stock.

"Well, keep it on at 74, then," instructs Losingsore. "Right"! says Angles, briskly. "Firm until cancelled you say?"

The next day, in the absence of any contract note in the morning's post, and on learning, to spur him further, that Prickett, similarly inspired, has bought himself *Twisters* at 75 Losingsore is onto his broker again.

Angles regrets he has been unable to get on, and that the price is now a penny either side of 76, with one jobber qualifying his quotation with "buyers only". "D'you want me to go higher?" he asks.

"Well, I don't know," hesitates Losingsore, lamely, feeling he is missing out on a "good thing". "Pay 77, then, but if you think it's worth going higher, I'll leave it to your judgment."

Around noon one of the jobbers contacts Angles to say that a line of *Twisters* has just come on offer at 78, and does his man want a thousand? "H'mm, he's supposed to have left it to me," ruminates Angles, warily. "Hold on a bit, I'll ring my client." But Losingsore is out at a prolonged luncheon.

"D'you think I'd be all right to go ahead?" queries Angles. "I can do the business at 78." Equally warily, the secretary supposes he might, and Angles buys a thousand.

Half an hour later the secretary's ringing back to say she's contacted Mr. Losingsore, and he thinks he'd better make it only five hundred. Angles appears headlong on the jobber's pitch just as the latter is marking down *Twisters* to 76 middle.

Learning in the commuter-compartment, on going home that evening, that Pricket has sold his *Twisters* at 78, Losingsore discreetly keeps his counsel.

"Snaffled a quick one, eh?" comments the Colonel. "Quite right too, m'boy. Y'know what I've always said, deal when you can!"

# Clearing a Path with a Ballpoint

"May I see Mr. Stockshort, please?" asks the visiting client, vainly appealing to the passing throng through the vestibule of some richly carpeted skyscraper office.

"Sorry, I'm afraid Mr. Stockshort's round at the bank," says a Good Samaritan, offering succour by the way. "Could the Head Statistician help?" The client forbids to remark that his partner is technically "In" on the office indicator board, but with the Head Statistician he has to be content.

This is so often the small investors' problem these days – pinning down their man. Relatively a few years ago, when they were religiously seeking initiation into the mystic rites of the Stock Exchange, it was different. Then the elusiveness of that essential professional contact – the stockbroker – was often the first hurdle. The pin was used speculatively in a wide arc over a short list of willing prospects obligingly provided on application to The Stock Exchange.

Now, with stockbrokers – or their scarcely reluctant minions – sprouting like herbaceous flowers in most of the better suburban roads, and having for some years enjoyed a personal service, it is rather frustrating to find one's private client identity being steadily submerged as just another cipher in the in'ards of some clinically clean computer.

Once was the day, and not so far past, when the broker-client relationship was a relaxed, intimate affair. The red carpet treatment was accorded the client offering the prospect of even a tenner's worth of commission. Top-hatted seniors would scurry from their warrens to regale their clients in Slaters, treating with the traditional glass of sherry, and inquiring benevolently of the wife and family.

But rollicking inflation, and 2.5 million direct investors besieging Throgmorton Street and its attendant outlets for the employment of their savings, have changed all that. With the cost of executing and processing each bargain anything from £12.00–£14.00, according to broking efficiency, portfolios of even £25,000 are taken on rather patronisingly these days. And Mr. Punt's contract for the purchase of 200 *Mirage Mining* (strictly limited to twenty-seven pence) is scarcely destined for the first-class mail.

This deluge of business has tended to submerge the personal touch. Part of the trouble is that broker-members, who formerly kept in close attendance on the market itself, have largely relinquished the rigours of the actual dealing to their agile aids. This is not wholly a matter of stamina, but equally the increasing demands of office administration.

It is the claim of many self-styled "experts", who adopt intermediate positions on the fringe of the market, that the stockbroker these days is far too busy with all the administrative chores to specialise seriously in advising clients. The argued superiority over the rigorously-controlled member-brokers lies in studious selectivity and pious impartiality, about both of which pretensions I personally have doubts.

The individual investor's estrangement, more and more, from his kindly mentor, the stockbroker, comes at a time, ironically, when he was never subjected to a greater deluge of advice. And never, accordingly, in greater need of a helping hand in clearing a path through the entanglement.

No, it is not advice that the investor is lacking; indeed, it is probably true to suggest that he is already hugely over-advised. Advice comes by the solid columnful, page after pageful, in supplements, journals, news letters, brokers circulars, statistical cards, even from the telly – all analysing, assessing, digesting, regurgitating, monotonously on and on.

The thirst for expertise, the urge for getting the supposed edge, knows no bounds in this modern world of investment. Gimmickry is rampant; superfluous services superimposed on the already superfluous; rarified advice offered even in appraisal of those who presume to advise. No wonder the personnel selectionists are almost plundering the pushchairs.

I often wonder how, should we ever attain the ultimate in sophisticated private investment, clients will ever get through finally to their stockbrokers? Will they expire on the way, ballpoint clasped resolutely in hand, from sheer exhaustion? Or will they, more likely, have got thoroughly fed up by then with the whole mind-boggling business?

Indeed, in this bewildering investment scene of over-advice, overlaid tiers of "experts", and taxgatherers busybodying from the cradle to the grave, many are beginning to yearn for the simple life again – the glass of sherry treatment, and – "What about a couple of thou of *Barnacle Bakeries*, Old Boy?"

However, with the sherry liable to have been replaced by a plastic beaker of indescribable coffee from the office Hot Drinks vendor, and the client's particular partner interminably "round at the bank", he may regard himself now as neither cordially regailed nor intimately informed.

To suggest that this situation is the resounding cue for organizers of channels of indirect investment is scarcely original, I know. Investors are already well aware of the advantages of the "packaged" investment, which removes the headaches of selection, supervision, and, to a large extent, the impenetrable mysteries of Capital Gains Tax, all in one go, for the weary and perplexed.

Call it gaining converts on the rebound, if you like, but this urge for simplicity is precisely what is going increasingly to reinforce the ranks of the unitholders in the years ahead.

# I Picked my Broker with a Pin

I've got myself a stockbroker. *"My broker"* – it is surely almost a "high" in status symbolling? *"I'm* just dropping round on *my* brokers," I can airily let fall in the office. *"My* broker recommends *Canalized Canals."*

I took the step recently on receiving the final instalment of my late grandmother's estate. At that stage, it seemed, my affairs called for a more direct supervision than could be expected from the bank. I therefore wrote, as frequently advised in the papers, to the Secretary, The Stock Exchange, London E.C.2, asking to be put in touch with a broker.

The response was a short-list of six firms from which to pick. Confronted impersonally by a list of mere names, it is hard to decide where one's interests are likely to be best served. Messrs. D'Arcy, McGitten, FitzWilliam, of Palatial Buildings, for example, sounded a bit pretentious for my purse. There were 15 partners and six telephone numbers on the letter-heading. I could hardly imagine Mr. D'Arcy descending to the level of 100 *Spinning Top Traders*, at eight pence apiece.

On the other hand, take Prodnose, Rake and Turdy, of Swill Alley – a plebeian ring about them, if you like, although I was a bit dubious about the address. I studied the name combinations a bit longer. I had the idea of putting them into order of preference, like a slogan competition. In the end, however, I waved a pin in a wide arc and drove it down firmly into the "o" of Burging, Upshaw, Prout, of 5 Chance Lane.

If the method of choice was impetuous, the result was satisfactory. I was most amiably received – on paper – by Mr. Upshaw. He sent a copy of the firm's last circular, a monthly investment list that must have cost fifty pence, answered questions covering my 18 separate investments and purchased, on my behalf, 85 *General Engineering Industries*, which bargain he unfortunately had to undo the following day, as I had meant (a fact I attempted to explain) 75 *General Engineering (Radcliffe)*.

This slight misunderstanding apart, I was so delighted with my reception that I decided to call in person and make the acquaintance of the senior partner. There is nothing like personal relationship in business.

Chance Lane is reputedly just off Throgmorton Street. It sounded simple enough to find. In fact, I discovered that "off" encompasses a square quarter-mile of brokers' warrens bounded on the east by Throgmorton Street and on the west by London Wall.

I located number 5 and climbed a flagged stairway grasping a gaunt iron handrail. "Look out, sir!" shouted someone. It seems that cleaners habitually lurk in City buildings to ensnare the unwary. This one had deposited his bucket plumb in the centre of the landing.

I continued up to the third floor where a monstrous hand painted on

*I felt like the invisible man standing there*

a wall pointed imperiously the way to, among other occupants off a long corridor, the offices of Burging, Upshaw and Prout. On one of the many glass-panelled doors I found their "General Office".

Those of you who have entered a stockbroker's office for the first time will know the sense of being suspended in a sort of vacuum. Personally, I felt like the Invisible Man. Standing there, in the inner passage, staff passed around and beyond, apparently oblivious to my presence. I hesitated as to what I should do – cough or look lost.

But let me impart a tip. I have since discovered that one unfailing recognition signal is to display a cheque. I learnt this because, for want of something better to do on this occasion, I nervously took out the statement of account for my 75 *General Engineering* and the cheque in settlement. From nowhere a clerk swooped on me like a hen harrier.

I explained that I had an appointment.

"Oh, I'm so sorry, sir," said the clerk, tonelessly (he had by then looked at the statement). "Mr. Burging is off ill. He thought he'd take a day at home."

"I imagine he got my letter?" I asked.

The clerk imagined so.

"Perhaps Mr. Upshaw, then?" I ventured.

But Mr. Upshaw, it seemed, was dealing in the House, and might be some time. Mr. Prout, as a last resort? So sorry, Mr. Prout was inexplicably delayed over lunch, although it was then fully 3.15.

"The head statistician will see you, sir." The clerk was suddenly quite positive. "I'll tell him."

The head statistician, the client will quickly discover, is the invariable stand-in for the partners, the buffer, go-between, maid-of-all-work. He answers a great deal of the firm's correspondence, anyway, shapes the investment policy, knows most of the clients, and – most important – is always at hand.

The statistician greeted me affably, took me into his office, and sat me down behind a desk loaded with investment schemes and copious calculations on scraps of paper.

"The partners will be truly sorry to have missed you," he apologised. "Will you have some tea?"

I had tea, and a useful half-hour's chat (so far as the telephone would allow) on the election prospects, devaluation, the nationalization of steel, and might I have half-commission for re-investment if I sold 15 *Channel Tunnel* against my purchase of the *General Engineering*? I then took 14 *Extel* statistical cards on companies I had been considering, and departed. The statistician looked a trifle strained, I thought, as he bade me goodbye. These people are much overworked, I fear.

Although I did not have the pleasure of meeting either Mr. Burging or Mr. Upshaw, I rather fancy I may have almost bumped into young Prout hurrying up the passage as I left the office. I couldn't be sure, because he dived into a door marked "toilet".

# He Who Hesitates is Lost – or
# Mr. Prickett's lament

Most stockbrokers will be all too familiar with what one might call the "dead-end dealer" – the procrastinating, potential seller who wantonly runs himself into the last extremity of the Stock Exchange Account before closing up a speculative position.

"About your thousand *Miracle Mining*," his broker will tentatively prompt on the Tuesday before the Account-end. (Unless he cannot help it he's not going to let his client play straight into the hands of a reluctant market at the eleventh hour on the following Friday afternoon.)

"They're down five pence you know," his broker presses. "Do you intend to take them up?" A flattering suggestion, this. Mr. Prickett has already proved singularly unresponsive to several accounts rendered for a twenty-six pounds difference incurred on an earlier flutter. And *Miracles* are priced in the hundred and thirty pence range.

The Eternally Hopeful is expectantly evasive. "Oh, I don't know," he falters on the other end of the line. "I'll probably let them go, I think. But leave it a couple of days; they're bound to pick up."

His broker has no such conviction about the market's obligation to Mr. Prickett, but does not press the point.

On Thursday, when the broker sees fit to remind his client that nothing miraculous has yet been manifest, Mr. Prickett is still obstinately inspired by a faith in imminent recovery.

Come dead-end Friday, and the shares lamentably losing another tenpence it's no longer a matter of pious hope, but of dire necessity, that the client should hang on.

"They can't go worse," he consoles himself. "Better wait until this afternoon." (Oh, can't they,, thinks the broker!)

At 3.15, when the broker 'phones in final desperation, trying vainly to catch an early train to Bournemouth, they have gone worse – inevitably. After all, the broker's been bobbing up on the particular jobbers' pitches for the past two days with the regularity of a dextrously handled Yo-yo.

"Well, couldn't you get a bit more?" pleads the client. "You said they were a hundred and twenty-four pence bid this morning.'

His broker regretfully points out that that was this morning, that he has missed his lunch, looks like missing his train, and the best he can possibly squeeze now, five minutes before the "Close", is twenty-two pence. And he'd better be quick about it, too.

"Oh!" laments the client, lamely. "I wish I'd known."

The broker deals to bump up the client's debit balance to close under the three hundred mark, about which he has considerable misgivings.

"Deal when you can," is a good old Stock Exchange axiom, and is doubly true when, as the potential seller of a speculative holding, it is also a matter of when you must. The other great truth, of course, is that when cutting a loss, the first cut is invariably the cheapest.

If you are "in" for the Account, particularly in the sort of "thin" markets lately experienced, be sure the jobbers have a shrewd idea of what cards are out, among whom, and when they are going to be played. They are not there to extricate the speculators.

In conditions such as these, when you are possessed of a speculative and highly tenuous profit, you will almost certainly be in company, which means that somebody else will beat you to the sale unless your broker has early and decisive instructions. The tactics of "wait-and-see" can only lead fatally to the dead-end disposal.

On the other hand, when markets have a steadily rising momentum, there is enough genuine business passing to obscure the wholly speculative endeavours. Advance buying for each New Account may then provide a springboard on which the short-term operator can extricate himself.

# Prophet

Jimmy Punt is now retired to the end of a long pier on the South Coast where, with the only aptitude he's got – of talking – he tells fortunes, but takes remarkably good care that they haven't the remotest chance of coming true.

For example, to the sentimental sexagenarian, who can barely crawl over the door step, he predicts marital bliss with a teenage sports mistress; to the virgin spinster in pebble glasses, the gift of quadruplets; and so on.

He hopes, in this way, to avoid the tragedy of his punditry in the City.

Many investment advisers strive a lifetime in seeking acclaim for their acumen; with Jimmy, the mantle of Midas enveloped his narrow frame within a matter of hours to invest him with an entirely undeserved reputation.

Jimmy had gravitated to the stock market at the age of twenty by way of six months with a unit trust and an even briefer sojourn with a merchant bank. He then answered an advertisement for a Personal Assistant in a stockbroking firm. This offered £9000 a year, plus fringe benefits, for the modest requirement of "some experience".

Jimmy's qualifications being adequate enough, he got the job and was installed in the dealers' musty little cubicle situated, as it seemed, halfway up the chimney, with the firm of Openshaw and Clamp. There he was entrusted with the affairs of a number of unwitting investors while the senior partner, Mr. Clamp betook himself to the Bahamas.

The firm was small, and relied for its bread-and-butter on the junior partner, Triffitt, whose brother was secretary to an investment trust.

By keeping his eyes and ears open, and assiduously picking as many brains as he could, young Punt quickly began to build up a little half-commission business of his own.

His discoursed loudly, and often imprudently, with his fellow-commuters on the 8.12, which he found a useful field for expanding his clientele.

Attempting to alight with agility – and too early – at Waterloo one morning, he was firmly repulsed by a diligent porter. With the carriage door slammed smartly back on his foot, the young man's audible anguish prompted an elderly occupant – none other than the chairman of a prominent publicity group – to look up vaguely over the edge of his financial paper.

"What's that, m'boy? *Flushing Hall*, did you say? Are they a good buy? Must make a note of that."

When Jimmy hobbled painfully into the office decidedly late that

*All hell let loose*

morning, after an enforced stop at a hospital outpatients' department, he found all hell let loose. Telephones were shrilling on every hand, the office boy was actually awake, and the manager reduced to the verge of hysteria.

"Oh, Mr. Punt, thank goodness you're here," he cried, wringing agitated hands. "Everybody's wanting you. Mr. Triffitt's had to go down to the market to help out the dealer. And you know how he likes his glass of sherry about now. It's all that *Flushing Hall*."

"The property developers, you mean?" questioned Jimmy, in bewilderment. "What about them?"

"But surely you know, sir?" The manager sounded incredulous. "You tipped them to all your friends. They're being taken over. It was announced shortly after the market opened. My word, what a killing! The shares are up fifty pence."

Jimmy had the presence of mind to gulp twice. He was a bright lad, and had learnt the wisdom of playing for time when he didn't know what the heck was happening.

"Ah, *Flushing Hall!*" he fumbled. "Why, yes, of course, *Flushing Hall.*"

Seeing the light, he dived in at the deep end. "Well I must say. I wasn't expecting the news so quickly," he added.

"Brilliant information, I must say," enthused the manager. "Let me know your next good thing."

Jimmy was just about expanding under the admiring gaze of the office when a clamorous phone was thrust into his hands. It was the elderly gentleman in the corner seat with fulsome thanks. Apparently he had bought 2,000 shares directly the market opened, and was pleading for more inside information. Recklessly advising *Spilby's Sausages*, which was the first share to spring to his mind, Jimmy dived for the next telephone.

He was kept literally on the hop all day. The confidence of his fellow-travellers had spread like a prairie fire. Recklessly, in his efforts to placate ardent followers, poor Jimmy tipped off the cuff, dropping share names he knew not where, like a distraught magpie ransacking a duchess's jewel-box.

Unfortunately the market was in buoyant mood and he inadvertently hit on a succession of further winners.

Unfortunately Clamp and Openshaw's facilities, in a building at whose door developers were already tentatively knocking, were quite inadequate for the avalanche of business unleashed by a Throgmorton Street Pied Piper.

Where Mr. Clamp, hurriedly recalled from his holiday, had at first been congratulatory, Jimmy detected after a few days a certain strain.

Mr. Triffitt, too, uprooted from the serenity of his little club round the corner, was becoming less affable. The staff, hurriedly increased with fatal consequences to the accounting system, wallowed impossibly in a sea of paper.

Wilting himself beneath the increasing spate of orders, Jimmy realized that he must somehow take off the heat or be hoist, so to speak, with his own prophetic petard.

The only way to do this, he sensed, was to go smack into reverse by tipping a colossal stumer.

The trouble was that with the way his recommendations were generating their own success, he couldn't be sure that he wouldn't once again hit the jackpot. Then, with a sudden flash of inspiration, he remembered Simon Loosestrife.

Simon had been his very first client and was employed by a firm of systems analysts. He worked out all his share selections on a clinically actuarial formula.

And never once, as Jimmy could recall, had he ever picked a winner. Indeed, their connection had terminated with Mr. Clamp insisting on the closure of the account after a long standing debit from calamitous speculations.

Jimmy felt sure Simon would not fail him. Heartened, he rang up right away.

"Is that you, Simon? Punt here. I say, I suppose you haven't got a good thing on the market? I'm simply desperate for a real winner."

He heard ironic laughter on the other end of the line.

"Wouldn't have thought so." Simon chuckled. "From what I hear, you've hit everything in the list worth buying."

"That's just it," admitted Jimmy, hoping to sound sufficiently despondent. "I've run out of ammunition. Come on, you're never short of an idea."

And, as it turned out, Simon wasn't. He'd just finished an exhaustive research into *Cannon Canisters*. The very thing, he said: year's profits due any day, and certain to have made a bomb. He was so confident, he said, that he had bought himself 1,000.

Jimmy hugged himself; Simon usually ventured in a couple of hundred which was disastrous enough.

"Well, what do you know?" chanted the commuter-compartment next morning, and Jimmy, in unabashed response, talked *Cannon Canisters* solidly until the 8.12 hit the buffers at Waterloo.

On the strength of his past successes, Jimmy's ardent followers bought with unequalled appetite. And they were not disappointed. A few days later *Cannon Canisters* published its results. They were a headline hit – profits erected out of the deepest red to a bounding black dividend restored and handsomely earned, free share bonus – the lot. The share price doubled overnight.

Which explains why Jimmy is now so meticulously careful in his fortune telling.

His kiosk is right at the end of the pier, and it is an unpleasantly long way over.

# "Well, what d'you know . . .?"

Of all the many elements in the make-up of the stock market, information is not the one most conspicuously lacking in the region of Throgmorton Street. There are always willing locals prepared to pour into the attentive ear, sizzling hot news on any matter, from gold to groundnuts, *War Loan* to *Winkelhaak*.

Their formula is "What d'you know?" A lot of people ask it in the City. It has come, with long usage, to be almost a ritual greeting – "Morning, Old Boy, what-d'you-know?"

It's a subtle opening, if you come to think about it: it puts the questioner in the role of clueless supplicant, while flatteringly crediting the questioned with having a little something up his own sleeve.

The victim, when constrained to admit that he knows not a sausage, Brazil or otherwise, is forced from politeness to return the compliment. And here is where he makes his mistake.

"Ah, I'm glad you asked," the Much Informed will whisper, glancing mysteriously around. " 'Fact is, I can let you in on something good. Strictly off the record, y'know. Got it from my accountant friend on the eight-twelve. The one who gave me *Ross Group*." He then breathes heavily into his listener's ear.

Newly Informed gasps, incredulously. "Not *Slipstitch Knitwear*?"

"None other. At eighty pence, he tells me."

"Does he know for certain?"

Much Informed hesitates. "Well, I wouldn't care to say certain. Fairly certain, anyway."

It can sometimes emerge, if the font of knowledge is relentlessly tapped, or rendered less positive by proffered refreshment, that his wife's cousin honestly believes so, from what she can gather from her boyfriend, who works for the company's branch office.

But, on the other hand, assuming the hook thus juicily baited is greedily swallowed, the finessing move is the deliberate underplay. The hand seems virtually thrown away.

"But, look here," Much Informed will add anxiously, "promise you won't buy many. Interfere with the market, and the deal could be off." The other version of this one is to blandly dismiss the rosy prospect as of academic interest only, since the shares are already "buyers only".

Either way, Newly Informed will then passionately protest his discretion to the grave, and undoubtedly speed off, like a greyhound from the leash, to buy three times as many shares as he originally intended.

The truth about "information" is that ninety per cent of it is either opinion masquerading as fact or hearsay descending past the piously sealed lips of successive elaborators, from half-truth to fantasy.

Unfortunately, in these days of bids, leaks and inquests, information

*The one who gave me 'Ross' group*

has come to be suspect as much for what it could be, as for what, ten-to-one, it is not. Which is liable to put the recipient, who has heard it all before and invariably lost his shirt, in the ironical position of perhaps picking a pearl of wisdom too hot to handle.

"Sorry I put you on to a stumer," apologises Much Informed a few days later.

"Why the sorrow?" protests the expansive punter. "They're up ten bob. Thanks, very much."

"But haven't you heard? There's a Council inquiry."

Investors who are prudently shy of the alleged "good thing" may alternatively subscribe to the oft-quoted assumption that there is seldom smoke without fire. Which makes the stock market these days confusingly like a glass-strewn heath on a broiling July Sunday.

The unfortunate thing about smoke signals is that the more company chairmen leap around, attempting to quench their respective conflagrations, the more they unwittingly fan the flames. "Ah, he's only trying to hide something," mutter the speculators sagely. Which only goes to prove, as I always contend, that with the best will in the world, markets are not so much what things are, as what investors choose to think they are.

# Fair Shares

Melvyn Stockbull, to put it politely, was a purveyor of stock market advice. You may have seen the fruits of his or similar labour caustically referred to in the financial columns – *"Spillby's Spindles* rose on a West End tip" – or something similar.

He cast his seed with practised charm around the plusher hotels from Torquay to Troon, where salt sea breezes, far removed from inhibiting proximity with statistical fact, give refreshing speciousness to financial opinion.

Some of this seed took root to the enrichment of Melvyn and his syndicate. Some other fell astray. I relate of one such wayward seed.

I met Melvyn in the faded grandeur of a stucco-fronted monstrosity of an hotel at Strandshingle Bay. He was a charming young man, whose sports coat pockets sprouted financial literature with the artless abandon of the enthusiastic investor.

It was I who first accosted him, so disarmingly innocent was our meeting. It was certainly I who raised the subject of shares.

He was conspicuously reading the *Financial Times*, that unfailing recognition signal for a coveted exchange of "shop", when I entered the hotel bar.

Where you can't say blatantly, "Excuse me, do you happen to hold *Consolidated Twisters?*," you can with dignity inquire of a fellow-guest, "Might I glance at your Pink Un, sir? They've sold out at the shop."

I ordered a gin-and-tonic and did just that. Melvyn obliged with courtesy. We talked briefly of the weather, and then inevitably, as men do on holiday, we passed to business.

Melvyn, as it came out, was an accountant, junior partner with an eminent firm whose admonishing finger was enough to make erring chairmen quake. He was snatching a few days' breather, he told me, from auditing the books of a public company.

I asked indiscreetly were they quoted on the market?

"Well, I shouldn't tell you," confided Melvyn in impressively lowered tone. But he did. "It's *Tingley's Slipwear* – you know, the women's underwear people."

I did indeed. It was difficult not to know the firm unless you were both deaf and blind; it was engaged just then in an immense sales drive. Its slogan – "Slinkily in Tingley's" – shrieked from every newspaper, hoarding and TV set.

"They must be spending a fortune," I suggested invitingly.

"Spending!" Melvyn cast suppliant eyes to heaven. "You can't imagine. Sales are going like a bomb."

"Sounds healthy," I admitted.

And healthy it was, I gathered. He didn't tell me as much right away, but after a couple more gins-and-tonics, went on to convey that the coming accounts would show a boom in profits, with a bumper share bonus in the offing.

What more could one possibly want – coming straight from the auditor.

We didn't talk any more then as the dinner gong went, but I suspected from cosy chats Melvyn engaged in with several elderly ladies and retired military gentlemen who inhabited the lounge that we quickly shared a common confidence. Whether or not we were equally enjoined to discretion on the delicate subject of *Tingley's*, we certainly kept our respective counsels. But I did notice after that an increasing eagerness to intercept the morning papers.

In any case, what happened next dispelled any musty atmosphere of mere pounds and pence that may have lingered in our midst with a heady waft of expensive Paris perfume.

It was the arrival of Miss Lilian Plinnith, whose matching luggage we watched piled to the size of a miniature pyramid in the hall, and whose expanse of shimmering leg transported the page into a reverie from which he had to be crudely pinched to consciousness by the head porter.

Apart from the page, we all succumbed to the allure of the new guest – not least the amicable Melvyn. What she was doing at such a dead-end spot, we couldn't imagine. Something was let fall about a strained cartilage.

From the moment of her arrival Melvyn was her earnest swain. They bathed, boated, and romanced together, so far as we could see, the livelong day. And what we couldn't see we hinted at in undertones.

For the next twenty-four hours I naturally didn't see much of Melvyn. Then on the following evening he suddenly button-holed me in the bar with every evidence of urgency.

"Look here," he whispered, "about *Tingley's*. Remember what I told you about them doing well?"

I assured him of my recollection.

"Yes, I know," he said with some confusion. "Well, I hope you didn't buy any, that's all. The fact is I've been on the blower to-day to my clerk who's working in their offices. He tells me the latest profit figures are sharply down. The cost of his advertising seems to be clipping margins."

I said I was surprised business fortunes could change so quickly.

"Profits are very marginal in the rag trade," he explained vaguely. "I

*From the moment of her arrival Melvyn was her earnest swain*

wouldn't like to see you lose. It could be embarrassing for me in my position."

I thanked him for his solicitude, and assured him that I had not bought any *Tingley's* shares. At which he seemed greatly relieved.

"Not that there's anything seriously wrong," he added hurriedly.

Whether Melvyn was able to set the record straight with our fellow-guests I simply didn't know then. In the case of old Miss Limley, anyway, he couldn't have done so. She was still a blissfully optimistic shareholder if she had bought any, for the simple reason that she had gone away only the day before for a long weekend.

The reason for Melvyn's violent change of opinion didn't become apparent until after dinner the next day, which was Sunday. We were all in the lounge lingering over coffee when Miss Limley, who had returned unexpectedly early, suddenly joined us.

She tottered straight up to Melvyn, who was squeezed on a sofa in restricted proximity with Miss Plinnith, and commenced to thank him with undisguised delight for the wonderful tip he'd given her.

If looks could have silenced, Melvyn's mute, impassioned glare would have struck the good spinster dumb on the spot. But she was too far launched in her thanks to have heeded even an atomic bomb. It seemed not only had she bought some shares, but by a happy coincidence they had gone up quite sharply the previous Friday.

"Dear boy, no modesty!" she admonished gushingly. "I do believe I've made at least twenty pounds. All thanks to you."

The rest of us returned our coffee cups inaudibly to their saucers in an atmospheric silence. Miss Plinnith drew in her breath sharply. But this may have been due partly to the fact that Melvyn suddenly shot up from the sofa on recollecting he had left his cigarettes in his room.

Then Colonel Millblank added fuel to the fire by exploding.

"But he told me, dammit, the blankety things weren't worth buying after all!"

This was too much for Miss Plinnith, propelled to her feet by the suddenness of Melvyn's departure. She confronted us in mini-skirted wroth.

"Look, I'd like to know," she demanded hotly, "what that young man's been telling you? I'd like to know," she added caustically, "because I happen to be a member of *Tingley's* board."

We all gaped at this surprising revelation.

Suddenly I saw the light.

"Did you tell him that?" I asked.

The girl hesitated.

"Well, I don't spread it around. But, yes. Yesterday after we bathed. We were getting along so nicely," she added wistfully. "He asked me what I did. He seemed so interested in business."

We were all most embarrassed, of course, but when we explained what had happened, she immediately saw we had been the unwitting victims of Melvyn's practised and plausible tongue.

"Well, perhaps it's lucky for you I'm here then," she said settling down. "The way you've all had this tale about *Tingley's* twisted topsy-turvy, I feel the least I can do now is to put you right."

Then she took us into her confidence.

"So you see," she ended, "Melvyn happened by luck to be right in the first place. *Tingley* shares really are well worth buying."

So there it was, for the first time in our lives, information from the inside. We secretly congratulated ourselves for being on to a "good thing".

"But you must treat what I've told you in strictest confidence," Miss Plinnith warned us.

Both of them left next day, Melvyn before breakfast.

Whether we all observed the confidence, I can't say. I certainly tipped a wink to my broker-friend on the 8.22, and *Tingley's* rose further after that by fifteen pence. I was standing to make a couple of hundred. A week later I was showing a substantial loss.

After that I looked up Miss Plinnith in the *Directory of Directors*, but strangely her name did not appear.

# Eustace and Amos

Cousin Eustace resides in town because, as he always insists, it is so vital to keep in constant touch with affairs. His stockbroker, in jocular mood, frequently affirms that were Eustace permitted a camp-bed in the office, the early clerk, turning key in lock, would assuredly find him dressed and eagerly awaiting events, on the other side of the mat.

Denied this ultimate vantage point, however, he does manfully what he can with a flat in the Barbican, the telephone, copious financial literature, and a daily visit to the clients' waiting-room.

". . . and you'll let me know if there's any change?" Eustace regularly requests, on dragging himself away from the magnet of the intriguingly changing price board.

A harassed clerk, juggling impossibly with three telephones, religiously reassures him. But as Eustace's current concern is *Tipplewhite's*, in course of a violent whirl in the stores section on takeover rumours, the young man's willingness to oblige stretches credulity a trifle far.

Eustace has lavished many a spread ingratiating himself with all the pundits of the day, so when he is not acclaiming the acumen of this or that confidant, in their inevitable moments of achievement, he is hopelessly befuddled by the range and variety of their proffered plums.

His cousin Amos, on the other hand, preferring the detached viewpoint, vegetates in deepest Dorset. Equipped with gumboots, in negotiation of the puddles down the lane, he penetrates no further than the postbox in the hedge, and economises by using the second-class mail.

Amos invariably takes a balance-sheet, instead of a biscuit, in bed with his early tea. Reclining at ease, he reads, assimilating all the succulent morsels of information, probing critically behind the small print, salting away facts and figures for future reference that might well escape the more rapacious researcher ransacking the share lists.

For all his cousin's close surveillance of the financial scene, the ardent pursuit of what he dignifies his portfolio, it is perhaps true to suggest that the pedestrian Amos is the better rewarded for being insulated from the sharper impact of events.

"Your cousin always seems to hit the jackpot," ruminated their broker, somewhat tactlessly, after the bid for *Tipplewhite's* had been duly announced, but painfully for Eustace at ten pence below the price to which the shares had been ambitiously hoisted.

Eustace adroitly asked but wouldn't *Marsh and Parcels* now stand a chance of a bid? Unfortunately, unlike *Tipplewhite's*, his broker pointed out, they didn't enjoy the luxury of a freehold corner site on a suburban broadway behind which, at a distance of no more than three hundred yards, was a greyhound track – a fact cousin Amos had apparently

*No further than the post-box in the hedge*

elicited from the asides of the stadium's chairman a year earlier, in touching briefly on the possibilities of re-development.

Possibly the trouble with the over-informed is that they are likely to have too many alleged "good things" piled on their plates. In picking about like a distraught magpie in the duchess's jewel-box, the chances are that they will drop the goodies in the confusion, only to end up disappointingly with the deceptive baubles.

# Never Mind the Figures – What about the Gin?

It was the day before the big event, the company news on which a dispirited market could pivot – the third quarter's figures of Mammoth Textiles. From the opening of the market, jobbers have advised that the vital announcement is scheduled for between 12 and 12.30.

This leaves at least two nail-biting hours of inactivity, in which the jobbers mark their prices up, mark them down or leave them where they were, while the rest of us take a leisurely coffee break.

Come the magic hour of noon, and a crowd of expectant brokers, dealers, "blue-buttons", and what-have-you, assemble beneath the Video-Scanners – in plain English, the main company news display screens.

Everybody is on tiptoe, furtively eyeing his neighbour, and measuring the distance to the nearest telephone.

The jobbers' duplicated proformas, conveniently setting out previous equivalent figures and giving parallel space for the impending revelations, have long since been devoured by brokers with the appetite of a swarm of locusts. These invaluable memoranda are now being twisted to shreds in nervous fingers.

Every warning buzz on the subsidiary Annunciator screens (these disclose sundry snippets of information from behind what appears to be a discreetly elevated bathroom blind) prematurely alerts the market.

The more agile leap for reassurance round corners to get a view of the latest revelation. But it is only Spoofamundulla Tea passing its dividend.

"Buy, buy, buy!" choruses the crowd – or groans with derision.

It is now 12.30 and near the deadline for table-bookings down in the Long Room. Then the *Mammoth* jobbers receive fresh advice and suddenly amend the time schedule. This is it, we assure ourselves. One o'clock, they say authoritatively, and write it big on their boards.

"Ah!" we breathe disbelievingly. We look speculatively at our watches, then towards the exits from the "floor". The crowd stirs instinctively ginwards.

"Nice time for a quickie," we calculate. It begins to look like a late sandwich for lunch. The crowd thins, leaving only the perversely incredulous.

Back judiciously by 12.45 – but too late. The display screens are already emblazoned with Mammoth's achievement. It came at 12.40, the midday traffic being less obstructive to the messenger's taxi than we imagined.

The figures beat the forecast by a massive margin, put the shares up 20p, and all the telephones in possession of abstinent competitors.

It really does look like a late sandwich with its edges unpalatably curled up.

# Dealings Suspended

If only Mumley had radio-telephoned his Sydney stockbrokers five minutes later he would never have landed himself with ten thousand *Moonshine Nickel* shares on an atoll in the Coral Sea. Not that he would have telephoned at all, in that case, because as he put down the receiver, Lord Erthump's luxury motor yacht collided at speed with some submerged wreckage, and promptly parted company with her bottom.

Mumley, one should explain at this critical point, always used to boast that his undoubted success as an investor was due to his keeping in constant touch with the market.

It was regrettable, therefore, that he should have succumbed, on an impulse, to his host's fulsome advocacy of *Moonshine* over a rather heady luncheon that very day. Indeed, if there was ever a share that needed watching, it was *Moonshine*.

Had it not been that his Lordship was the company's chairman, and had let fall increasing indiscretions about an unpublished nickel find as the meal progressed, Mumley would have weighed the prospects more critically.

As it was, what with the brandy circulating freely, it had seemed too much of a good thing to miss.

The wily Glubenthal, wizard of the takeover field, was close behind him in the queue of guests for the telephone when the yacht struck. Luckily the instrument was right next to the companion-way. With Glubenthal's girth impeding the rest of the frustrated speculators, Mumley gained a double first – this time to the deck.

In the confusion of abandoning ship, there was no time to collect even the most cherished possessions – such as cheque-books and credit cards. It was like a scramble for a new share issue.

Mumley attached himself to the first life raft to hand, pulled the inflation cord, and launched himself to the elements with his Sydney broker's words, "Right, I'll put that in hand at once," ringing ominously in his ears.

Reckoning his broker bought at about the previous day's price of 330p, his commitment was roughly thirty-three thousand pounds. He mentally worked it out again, this time allowing for expenses, and it came to a few hundreds more. If he had been anywhere near a telephone, he would have got back, on second thoughts, and cut his liability to five thousand shares.

As he reached the point where the figures of his mental arithmetic danced in the heat haze before his eyes, the raft suddenly canted up in a flurry of foam, and he found himself abruptly deposited in two feet of small surf.

Sitting on the hot sand, he surveyed the chasing lines of incoming breakers, and saw what he took to be a porpoise. It rose up and resolved itself into Glubenthal, who struggled up and slumped beside him.

"I was thinking," said he, without ado, "you might like to lighten your load in *Moonshine*? I would have picked up a few myself – just an interest, you know, if we hadn't gone down just then."

Mumley masked his instant relief.

"Well, I don't know," he hesitated. "That borehole news may have leaked out by now. It could give a big boost to the shares. 'Fact is," he added daringly, "I've been regretting I didn't make it twenty."

As they haggled, the rest of the party, all carried by the same caprice of current, came bobbing at intervals out of the surf.

"All right," Mumley relented, a shade too hurriedly, "I'll let you have a couple of thou of mine – just as a favour, mind."

"At three-hundred-and-thirty pence," prompted Glubenthal, suspiciously.

The other gave him an anguished look. "You can't expect me to let you in at a loss. There're the expenses, you know."

They dealt at 335p, all-in.

"Cash settlement," demanded Mumley. He had remembered the cheque-book fortuitously in his hip pocket and fished it out none too sodden for salvage. Glubenthal completed their clerical needs by the discovery of his ballpoint.

Going furtively farther up the beach and behind some rocks, they dried out the cheque-book, leaf by leaf, on the hot sand. Making alterations for his own bank, Glubenthal wrote one out for six-thousand-seven-hundred.

Later that day, whilst scavenging among rock pools for indigestible edibles of manifest agility, and regretting the while he had not taken more advantage of Glubenthal's enthusiasm, Mumley saw the Countess Martelli approaching.

She commented pointlessly on the excellence of the weather.

"But it is rather worrying," she went on, "don't you think, being so hopelessly out of touch? I imagine we might be here for weeks. My affairs – well, I hardly dare think."

Mumley mentally marked up the price of *Moonshine* to 355p.

"I was never more content," he replied. "I have always found it most profitable to have a long perspective."

*"I'll let you have a couple of thou of mine . . ."*

The Countess, it then emerged, was also regretting the break in communications with Sydney. So after a little delicate negotiation, Mumley generously satisfied her hankering after a stake in *Moonshine* by unloading another three thousand of his own – this time at 348p.

There was resort to Glubenthal for the loan of his ballpoint on three further occasions that evening. As *Moonshine* by then were changing hands well above his purchase price, he was only too eager to oblige.

On the other hand, with his own holding depleted to a thousand shares, Mumley was beginning to wonder whether the others had not perhaps wrung some more information out of Lord Erthump while they were adrift.

He retired to a restive sleep. Glubenthal also had a troubled night. It may have been an attack of colic brought on by a surfeit of raw fish-food. He awoke in distinctly depressed mood, and tried to cut his holding to Susie Lightfoot, the ballerina, at fivepence under the previous night's close. A shrewd miss, she was prompted to remark that she had sold a thousand previously held only the day before, but would be prepared to repurchase at 340p. And did.

For several days the alternating fortunes of *Moonshine* provided a frenzied diversion from the tedium of life for the castaways. Poor Lord Erthump was so persistently interrogated on the whys and wherefores of his company that he eventually retired to the outermost reefs where, slipping on a jellyfish, he fell to a watery grave.

The chairman's demise came at an untimely moment for Mumley, who had just picked up most of his holding in *Moonshine* at what he judged to be the bargain price of 327p. Immediately they were unsaleable.

In the excitement of the moment, according to who had bought or sold, nobody noticed that a liner had climbed up over the rim of the world.

They all sprang around, signalling with their underwear, until somebody cried, "Light a fire!" and some objector promptly retorted "With what?" Mumley, by this time the principal debtor, jubilantly supplied the answer. "The cheques!" he cried. These were hurriedly retrieved from incredible recesses.

But the Banker, a stickler for the niceties, intervened.

"Just a moment, though," said he. "Shouldn't we have a clearance first? The differences between us can be squared with I.O.U.s."

In all the interchange of *Moonshine* shares between buyers and sellers, the cheques were found largely to cancel out, leaving differences which the ultimate losers pledged with large, white pebbles duly inscribed to this end.

When they had set light to this literal paper fortune, and generously stoked the flames with most of the ladies' flimsies and driftwood, the illuminated antics of the castaways would have attracted the notice of even a blind man.

Into the boat lowered to pick up the party, Mumley sprang first, and pushed to the bow. He was possessed with the single purpose of getting to the ship's telephone, and cutting his ten thousand *Moonshine* before news of the chairman's death got out and punctured the market. His companions followed more slowly, hampered by the weight of their I.O.U.s.

When Mumley finally got through to his broker, who was fortunately delayed late at the office, that gentleman sounded gleeful.

"I've been trying to get in touch with you," he chuckled. "You've had a lucky let off, I must say."

"Why?" choked Mumley, white to the gills. "Didn't you buy them then?"

"No, wasn't in time," came the reply. "Dealings in *Moonshine* were suspended on all markets, here and in London, half-an-hour after you 'phoned the other day. An irregularity with the accounts, as they say."

With scrupulous regard for the rules of the market, the practised dealers of the yacht's party all dutifully emptied their pockets over the liner's side. The I.O.U.s made quite a splash.

# It's the Settlement . . .

"We don't seem to have had your cheque yet," hints the broker over the 'phone to the habitually recalcitrant client.

(Of course, the broker jolly well knows he hasn't. He's rightly taken the precaution of checking with the firm's cashier before ringing. It's distinctly embarrassing to embark on the conventions of the cheque angling game only to discover that settlement was forthcoming that very morning, but the debit inadvertently not struck off the late-payers list.)

"I suppose it's the post again," he adds, more by way of a statement than a question, making allowance for all eventualities. At this stage the benefit of the doubt is well in the client's court.

To which tactful inquiry the replies can be as varied and ingenious as those of the bidden guests to the gospel feast.

"That's strange," one will say, incredulously. "But I posted it off to you last Thursday directly I got the statement of account. 'Tell you what, I'll have it stopped, and send you another." Good for another three days' credit, that one.

"So sorry, I only got back from Cannes this morning," another will explain. "Haven't had time yet even to glance at my mail."

Or – "Now, let me see, did I get your statement?" It's the good old mail again with a two-way traffic in misdirection which might seem, on reflection, stretching coincidence a bit too far. Anyway, the date of settlement, or alternatively whether the bargain is "for cash", is clearly specified on every contract note.

Others mislay their cheque-book at the back of the bureau, depart on a world cruise, or unavailingly pass over, according to the inspiration of the moment.

When the same folk are on the receiving end, by contrast, they would seem literally to camp out on the other side of their letter-boxes.

"But," persists the broker, "you haven't sent us your certificate yet. The Transfer Department can't clear your credit for payment with Clients' Accounts."

"Damn, I told my bank manager to send it along to you fully a week ago," explodes the client. "I wonder if you'd do me a favour and let me have a couple of hundred to be going along with?"

The broker forbids to suggest that the bank manager's evident reluctance to part with the scrip is perhaps explained by the client having a spanking big overdraft. He compromises between tact and prudence by sending a cheque for fifty on account. After all, the client has a wealthy aunt in precarious health.

Unlike Christmas, Settlement Day comes regularly once a fortnight, except for the occasional three-week accounts. So the business of who

*They seem literally to camp out on the other side of their letter-boxes*

pays who, what, when, might be supposed in the end to become a little wearisome.

In fact, the Stock Exchange, traditionally most conservative in its habits and rituals, as regularly rises to the occasion with the smiling morning face. Dealers laconically shrug their shoulders in explanation of a hesitant market.

"Oh, it's the settlement, you know!" they patiently explain over the 'phone to querying clients, as if it were a mild, if passing, complaint like the measles.

"It's all part of the mystique of the market that everyone metaphorically walks tip-toe until after noon on Settlement Day. By this witching hour, if nothing untoward has happened (and, by the way, it is not for years that a defaulting firm has been declared on a Monday), the house is reassured that everything has "gone off" satisfactorily. It nearly always does.

This simple faith in the midday magic has arisen since the internal settlement has been effected centrally in the Settling Room which closes, for this purpose at 12 noon on the day in question. Formerly it was the procedure for clerks to deliver difference cheques around the offices, a labour liable to drag on all day.*

For the client, it should be a chastening thought that, irrespective of what he may or may not do in the matter of finding his lost chequebook, his agent, the stockbroker, will unquestionably fulfil his obligation to the market promptly and to the letter of the contract.

---

* Reference here is to the old manual system of Account Settlement, operated almost unchanged for 100 years, but replaced in stages, and now completely, by the long-discussed, £16-odd million TALISMAN computerized central settlement.

# Shares that Got Away

Losingsore is one of those lamentably unlucky investors – at least, so he never tires of telling any unwary audience at the local. Like the reminiscent fisherman, with expansive gesture, he's always recounting the ones that got away.

Pick the right share and, ten-to-one, Losingsore's either bought them too late, sold them too soon, bought too few, or failed to buy them at all – although seriously intending to do so.

"After all, Cracklin's the chairman, y'know," he will explain, accepting a restorative brandy. "We sit on the same bench. Couldn't go wrong, could I? So what did I do? Clean forgot about it. Lost a packet, I can tell you."

The trouble with Losingsore's selections is that he uses all the right statistical weights and measures, but somehow they never seem to turn out right. Like the anxious novice in the kitchen, he's always taking a peek into the oven to see if his shares have risen.

By now his late Aunt Mildred's five-hundred legacy has been propelled in and out through his broker's books, on so many abortive hunches, that two sides of a client's account card have been filled up for a diminished credit of four-hundred-and-twenty-two pounds and the Chief Cashier's complaint of writer's cramp.

"Worth putting a bit into *Hemlock Holdings*, don't you think?" he rings up to ask his broker, having thoroughly made up his mind that it is. "For the long-haul, I mean?"

His broker tactfully mutters something he hopes will pass for approval without appearing agreement. Losingsore's always sincerely intending to "invest".

Now follows the customary fortnight of studious deliberation, provision of costly statistical cards, and copious correspondence, while he irrevocably makes up his mind.

"Buy me five hundred," he one day instructs, in a tone of final decision.

"Right, five hundred!" echoes his broker, disbelievingly. "By the way, you know they're up ninepence since we first spoke?" (Pregnant pause over the 'phone.)

"W-well, that's different. I'm afraid I didn't. Well, I don't know I really don't. Perhaps we'd better think again, hadn't we?"

But ever resourceful, he's back within a few days suggesting *Hardcorn Footwear* as a share in which one could hardly put a foot wrong, and if it wouldn't be any trouble, could they get him please the last report and accounts. So through the whole tedious business yet again, only to find, at the final fling, that *Hardcorn* have unaccountably dropped twenty pence, which inevitably prompts Losingsore to drop them like a hot coal.

There are many investors like Losingsore, for ever lamenting the missed opportunities, the fortunes that have narrowly eluded them, the prophetic pearls of wisdom that have fallen on fallow ground.

In final desperation, and not without a trace of cynicism, his broker once suggested a "put-and-call" option as the possible solution to this state of permanent indecision. But in that case, as Losingsore promptly pointed out, his abiding fear would be that the selection would remain rigidly unchanged, in which case he would worry himself to death over the double option money!

# Developments at Lane End

Where the tarmac surface of the lane deteriorated to a gravel morass, two ladies, heavily laden with Christmas shopping, picked precarious ways among a series of miniature lakes. Their respective country cottages nestled right ahead, amid dripping winter foliage, all very secluded, respectable, and profoundly uninviting.

"Expecting Martin home for Christmas, Eva?" asked one, unsteadily balanced on a rutted ridge. Before her companion had time to reply, there was a staccato roar from up behind them, and something immediately indefinable took the potholes at a rush.

"I think he's come," admitted Mrs. Weatherspout, wiping the splattered mud from her eyes. A sports car careered to a screeching halt halfway into her neighbour's front hedge. She waved a restrained welcome.

"Why, Martin, I hadn't expected you so early."

"Hallo, mother!" A youth whose attire veered between Carnaby Street and the City Club alighted with a bound, followed by an equally youthful companion, whose locks descended riotously over his orange collar.

"Hallo, Mrs. Hardiman, I've got a New Year tip for your husband – a right little rollicker."

Mrs. Hardiman politely said her season's greatings, and forbade to add that her husband had not yet got over his last little tip for *Cordite Compacts*, discarded at forty pence just before the takeover bid at ninety.

"Oh, by the way, this is Albie," Martin waved vaguely. "I hope it's all right bringing him down for the night?"

Mrs. Weatherspout gulped, mentally counted the mince pies, and cordially welcomed the unexpected guest.

"Well, what have you got there – the Yule Log?" remarked Albie.

Mr. Weatherspout, alerted by an ominous crack, was attempting politely to secrete fragments of a shattered gate-post behind the hedge but by this time Albie, oblivious, was rummaging in the back of the car. He emerged with copious rolls of cartridge paper, a portable typewriter, and two slim brief cases.

As this unlikely luggage was transported to the cottage porch, Martin explained to his father in a whispered aside.

"Albie Sigman, y'know – the whizz-kid. Very big in property. Up to his eyes in it. All go-go-go."

Albie had certainly whizzed to no mean avail: from a couple of Nissen huts in Stepney, he had leapt, in a bout of backstreet trafficking, to boss of *Spiral Investments*, floated to net him a fortune overnight. But Mr. Weatherspout, who confined his investments to the bluest of "blue chips", had never heard of Albie Sigman. As a concession to the season's claims to goodwill, however, he refrained from any instinctive comment.

The two young men spent the entire afternoon until early dusk moving mysteriously among the undergrowth with a surveyor's tape. The Weatherspouts watched them briefly from the drawing-room window.

"Whatever do you think they're doing, George?" asked Mrs. Weatherspout.

Her husband shrugged. "No accounting for the young these days," he confessed. "It might be some sort of modern rite, like Flower Power."

"Very damp, I should think," concluded his wife, resignedly. "I hope they change their socks." And returned to her culinary preparations.

"We'll have the Christmas tree after supper," announced Mrs. Weatherspout brightly at tea, as if that occasion were edible too. "I've asked the Hardimans round. Millie's back for the holiday."

It was tradition with the Weatherspouts to get the present-giving over on Christmas Eve. Then with the litter of wrappings stuffed discreetly into the log-box, and a quick nip round with the sweeper, it looked respectable enough for breakfast next morning.

The two young men did not appear to hear her.

"We're going into the dining-room to do some work, mother," Martin announced. "D'you mind?"

"No dear, we're having supper round the fire in here. So cosy, don't you think?"

Nothing was heard from the dining-room for two hours except the sporadic clatter of the typewriter. Curiously, Mrs. Weatherspout peeped in once; the table was a litter of documents and plans, and her son and guest too diligently occupied to notice.

"I must say, I'm surprised how hard young fellows work these days," Mr. Weatherspout grudgingly remarked. "I wouldn't have believed it, on Christmas Eve, too. D'you suppose they'll surprise us tomorrow by going to church?"

The climax of the evening came after supper, during which the two young men preserved a conspirators' silence. With the room prettily lit by the fairy lights on the Christmas tree, the fire crackling merrily on the open hearth, Mrs. Weatherspout sat everyone down, and officiated in the presentations, handing round parcels ranging from the flabby concealment of her husband's pullover to the precise enclosure of Millie Hardiman's bottle of scent.

Gaudy paper began to mount underfoot to the accompanying exclamations of feigned delight and surprise. Oh, just what I wanted! No, not another! How *did* you guess! You shouldn't, I'll get as fat as a house!

The word house seemed unconsciously to be just the right cue for Albie. The pile of parcels beneath the tree had vanished. At which point he suddenly jumped up, and dived a hand into his pocket.

"And now," he said, "I've got a little surprise for you."

"How kind," muttered everyone uncomfortably, because they had nothing for Albie in exchange.

"Not at all," beamed that gentleman, totally indifferent to the embarrassed silence. "I hope you won't hesitate to accept." And to mystify matters further he thrust into the reluctant grasp of Mr. Weatherspout and Mr. Hardiman a businesslike looking envelope.

Doesn't know his manners, thought Mr. Weatherspout, typing the address for a Christmas card. I might have known. And irritably slit open his envelope.

Both men simultaneously withdrew the contents of their envelopes. Each contained two pieces of paper – one obviously an official letter; the other – small, and coloured – as obviously a cheque.

If Albie had meant his presentation as a sort of Christmas cracker, it could hardly have gone off with a more resounding bang. From the mutually dropped jaws, and expressions of blank amazement, the cheques were big.

"Eighty thousand!" gasped both men in unison. "Here, what the devil's this, young man? If it's your idea of a joke, it's in pretty poor taste, I must say."

They really got into full cry after Albie, and it was only perhaps his strategic position behind an occasional table bristling with breakables that saved him from physical hurt. As it was, he stood his ground manfully.

"That's right," he assured them blandly, "you've got three acres between you. I'll give you a hundred and sixty thou for the lot, fifty-fifty, cash down. It'll make a charming little development – fourteen houses to the acre density, if I push it with the Ministry. Lane End Estate, I thought I'd call it."

After Mr. Weatherspout had been thoroughly abusive about the betrayal of his hospitality, not forgetting to drag in the gatepost and his neighbour's hedge, a modicum of realism was restored over a couple of

*It was his strategic position behind an occasional table bristling with breakables that saved him from physical hurt*

rounds of drinks, and a good hard look at the cheques drawn on *Spiral Investments*.

"Eighty thousand!" Mr. Hardiman was still echoing incredulously. "I only paid five ten years ago." And, of course, the womenfolk were doing some pretty quick mental arithmetic, and were already, in imagination, off on a buying spree down Bond Street. In the end, the logic of the situation seemed unanswerable.

"Ah, well," sighed Mr. Weatherspout, resignedly, "I'll get well out of it this time. I've always fancied a snug little nest in South Shropshire – near Ludlow, I think. Peace and serenity, you know."

"Ludlow, you say?" Albie snapped the bait like an avid pike. "The very thing!"

He leapt for his rolls of paper, and whipped out a site plan, jabbing at it enthusiastically with his finger. "Look, I've got a simply cracking little development just near Ludlow. All very respectable: density only eight to the acre – parklike, almost . . ."

# Losingsore and the Three Partners

"Successful investment," quoted the Youngest Partner glibly, "thus obviously denotes the achievement of the quintessence of sound information and statistical analysis brought to fruition by the application of correct timing."

He paused for breath, and glanced apprehensively at the New Client, whose investment portfolio, inscribed on a small sheet of violet notepaper, lay apologetically on the desk before him.

The New Client took the hint.

"I've been poorly advised, perhaps," he admitted.

Nothing loath, the Youngest Partner regretfully concurred. He was but newly returned from a course of instruction on Stock Exchange practice, and plaguey knowledgeable on the policy of balanced investment. He shook his head despondently.

"No, no, I'm afraid this won't do," he said. "You're too concerned with immediate income. Now, what you want is growth potential. Buy management and the rewards will automatically follow. These old, traditional heavies of yours, like *Manifold Canisters* . . . 6 per cent, I hardly think so. *Cannon Casters* . . . we couldn't go along with those."

When he really settled in, he wielded his biro to devastating purpose.

"Well, that's about it," he finally admitted, and handed back the list.

The New Client looked at it ruefully. "You mean, I should sell the lot?"

"That's the idea," said the Youngest Partner briskly. "Make a clean sweep – clear out the dead wood."

He surreptitiously pulled out his cigarette case, and prepared to move ginwards to the firm's boardroom.

"Tell you what I'll do," he said reassuringly, as he reached the door. "I'll prepare you a scheme of reinvestment for this little lot. Well, goodbye, Mr. Losingsore, goodbye. We'll get you on the right road, never fear."

The scheme, when it arrived two days later, seemed a trifle slight for the smart, stiff cover that enfolded it. It comprised two recommendations – *Supreme Supermarts* and *Flushpink Cosmetics* yielding between them an average of 2.1 p.c.

The New Client dutifully did the switch, and mentally charged the £200 cut on his disposals, plus £36 incurred in expenses, to experience cheaply bought. Chancing to be in the vicinity of the broker's offices shortly before settlement day, he personally handed in his old certificate. His arrival in the vestibule coincided with the passage of the Second Senior Partner, all starch and sobriety, trailed by a retinue of statistical minions. He stopped in his wake to shake hands.

"Losingsore, isn't it? Well, how are they treating you? Let me see what you're holding."

*The new client passed along the heavily carpeted vestibule*

*Nothing so Crude as a Tip*

The New Client proffered his slender portfolio. The Second Senior Partner glanced at it briefly, shook his head, and a chorus of respectful "I absolutely agree with you, sir" suddenly crystallized into a crisp, "But this is not for you, Losingsore. What you want is scope for recovery. Get into something at the bottom. I recommend *Trindalls Tractors*. Come along to the dealing room, we'll do it right away."

Once more the New Client watched as his dwindling capital was uprooted, at the expense of further jobbers' turns and commission, and replanted securely in the potentially fertile soil of *Trindalls Tractors*.

Hardly had the new transactions been completed than loomed in the doorway none other than the Senior Partner himself. From his carefully groomed head to his immaculately polished shoes he permeated an aura of bristling efficiency and a faint smell of Imperial Leather. His worshippers flocked about him.

The Presence strode purposefully up to the dealing desk amid a respectful hush. He took one look at the newly completed dealing butts, and gave a short, sardonic laugh.

"Damn nonsense!" he snapped.

"Sir?" muttered the Office Manager.

With a Napoleonic gesture the Senior Partner surveyed the assembly.

"What an investor of Mr. Losingsore's age wants," he announced, in a voice of Final Decision, "is a spanking good income. Something like *Manifold Canisters* and *Cannon Casters*, I would suggest."

Twenty minutes later the New Client passed out along the heavily carpeted vestibule, past the floral displays, the plastic walnut veneer panelling, out through the swing doors, still tightly clutching his old certificates. Dimly he was beginning to understand the principles of reinvestment.

# Dealings on the Kerb

"Swifty" Millar, as he was known among such society as would still stand him a drink, was one of those inveterate kerb crawlers, with a quick eye for the misplaced trifle.

Mrs. Fynly-Claver, on the other hand, had no such propensity either by nature or estate. Had she been Swifty, she would have stooped in her stride and secreted the envelope beneath her mink for a perusal of its contents in the privacy of some nearby retreat.

As it was, being on her way along Threadneedle Street to keep an appointment with her stockbroker, she abstractedly retrieved it and popped it into her handbag along with some transfers and certificates she was about to hand in.

Swifty, too, saw the envelope – but a fraction late. It lay for a second imperiously in the gutter, stiff, unsullied, and eminently important-looking. His flight like a hen-harrier from the heights was unluckily impeded by two briskly stepping bankers, between whose legs he emerged to be denied his prey by the descent of a black-gloved hand.

Momentarily nonplussed, Swifty watched Mrs. Fynly-Claver's rear end retreating down the pavement, and reproached himself for a professional lapse. He had an instinct about that envelope. As it wasn't in his possession, he decided to keep its finder in sight, not knowing what turns a fickle fate might offer.

Unaware of Swifty's covetous eye, Mrs Fynly-Claver sailed majestically into the vestibule of a towering, cement office block, and ascended to the fourth floor. There, engaged in rapt contemplation of a fire hydrant, he observed her to pass through the swing doors of Messrs. Timberling, Gramble, stockbrokers.

Requesting Mr. Champerlain, her man of affairs, Mrs. Fynly-Claver was shown ceremoniously into the client's waiting-room. Left to herself, she opened her bag and took out the envelope. Marked "Personal and Confidential", it was addressed by name to the chairman of *Manifold Plastics*. Mrs. Fynly-Claver elevated her eyebrows. She knew the company as the veritable giant amongst its kind.

Conscience wrestled briefly with curiosity – and lost. There being no means of subtlety, Mrs. Fynly-Claver committed the end of her ballpoint and unceremoniously ripped open the flap.

When she read the enclosure, her eyebrows elevated even higher. It was written by the chairman of the ailing *Plastrum Plastics*. Briefly it acknowledged receipt of *Manifold's* generous offer of acquisition, and intimated his board's willingness to accept the terms.

As she was digesting this literal gem for the second time, a secretary arrived to conduct her to Mr. Champerlain. So she abruptly replaced the letter and its envelope back among other papers in her bag.

*. . . denied his prey by the descent of a black-gloved hand*

Mrs. Fynly-Claver was one of those women who professed a profound disdain of such mundane matters as mere pounds, shillings and pence. Which meant, as her broker had learned from long experience, that she was a remarkably shrewd operator. But even he was mildly surprised when, after an exhaustive review of her investments, she expressed the intention of buying five thousand *Plastrum Plastics*.

"I have an intuition," she announced, vaguely, forestalling him on the evident point of protest. And not being a man prepared to deny the possibilities of that feminine attribute, Mr. Champerlain instructed his Order Room.

"I think they're about twenty-two pence," was all he said. "We'll see."

While they were seeing, Mrs. Fynly-Claver produced her documents, accompanied by some miscellaneous contents of her handbag, all over the desk. The signing of her transfers, attentively supervised by Mr. Champerlain, together with the recovery of a lipstick from the wastepaper basket, covered her departure in some confusion, but not before the purchase of five thousand *Plastrum Plastics* had been reported.

Meantime, gathering up his departed client's documents, Mr. Champerlain uncovered the letter. As he read its unmistakable message, he could almost feel the watchdogs of the City Code on Take-overs and Mergers breathing down his neck. It was pretty obvious from where it had come, and equally to whom it did not belong.

To suggest that Mr. Champerlain was profoundly embarrassed would be to put it mildly. His first impulse was to drop the unwelcome epistle out of the window. Then, remembering his unwitting complicity in his client's purchase, his second was to speed it on its appointed way, and that with alacrity.

Putting the letter in his pocket, he hurried to the typists' pool, and, after a discreet comparison of type styles, had a similar envelope addressed in the same form. Completing the substitution in his office, he sped out with less decorum than his position on the office letter-heading would have normally allowed.

Now, the patient Swifty, if nothing else, had a gift for putting two and two together. So when he saw an obvious principal, attired with much starch and sobriety, bolt from the offices of Timberling, Gramble clutching an envelope of familiar appearance with conspiritorial intent, he chanced the accuracy of his arithmetic and followed.

Mr. Champerlain made the short distance to the registered offices of *Manifold Plastics* in what must have been record time, and surreptitiously slipped the envelope on to the housekeeper's desk in the hall. Swifty, as surreptitiously, followed and noted its destination. He sensed it would be best not to intercept yet again.

After that Mr. Champerlain felt immensely relieved. He almost caught himself chuckling at what, as he saw, could well be a hoax. By the time he regained his office, he was convinced it *was* a hoax, and was so hugely amused at the credulity of womankind that he bought another five thousand *Plastrums*, as a sort of souvenir to mark the occasion.

The Dealing Room had no sooner reported his purchase than Mr. Champerlain's buoyant mood was rudely deflated like a pricked balloon. His secretary appeared to announce hesitatingly that a "man" had called. He was inquiring after Mrs. Fynly-Claver.

Mr. Champerlain immediately had visions of big boots and a bowler, and was only slightly appeased by Swifty's apparition in the doorway. But not for long.

"It's about the letter," announced the visitor, pointedly, still playing it very much by ear.

"Ah, the letter!" intoned Mr. Champerlain, dully.

"That's right, the one the lady left. You afterwards took it round to *Manifold Plastics*," Swifty supplied, obligingly.

"You saw me take it?" Champerlain's expression would have blighted a celestial choir. "You haven't got it, have you?"

Swifty mischievously patted his breast pocket.

"I might have," he admitted. "But then, again, I mightn't. We don't want to upset *Manifold's* business, now, do we?" He folded his legs comfortably. " 'Tell you the truth," Swifty continued, "I like *Manifold*. A better proposition, don't y'think? I wouldn't mind a couple of thousand of their shares, now."

"A couple of thousand!" repeated Mr. Champerlain, aghast. "Why, they're two-hundred-and-fifty pence a share."

"I know," replied Swifty, complacently. "That's what I mean – a better class of share. Yes, buy me a couple of thou. And, by the way," he added, getting up, "forget to send me the account, will you?"

Whether the letter was indeed a hoax, whether Swifty further diverted it from its course, or whether negotiations were finally broken off, were questions of abiding mystery to both Mr. Champerlain and his fair client. All that happened after that was that *Plastrums* went persistently down, and *Manifolds* relentlessly up.

Which was how Mr. Samuel Millar, as he is now known through the records of Messrs. Timberling, Gramble, got the start to his little investment portfolio.

He still does his business through the somewhat reluctant Champerlain. This he finds advantageous, as that gentleman, given an occasional nudge, regularly puts him on to the better things.

# How Can Mr Losingsore run his Broker to Ground?

Our inveterate investor Losingsore, to whom I have alluded more than once before, turns over his brokers like leaves in the autumn breeze – or certainly did when he could get them.

Once, pre-decimalization, he enjoyed the tolerance of top-hatted senior partners, who could even be cajoled into a round of golf of a precious Saturday morning. That was in the dear, dead days of "three-two-six" (colloquialism for ¾d. commission on 1,000 shares), when some principals would dutifully attend in Slaters, to stand a glass of sherry and personally do the dealing.

Nowadays, however, with the cost of processing a share transaction having rocketed to, on an average, £13 a time, the senior partner of his latest victim regales himself around the boardrooms of the nearby merchant banks, and has never heard of Losingsore, who does his best, anomalistically, through the dealing box, where he submits to the services of half-a-dozen harassed clerks.

Losingsore was always one of those quick to resort to pen and paper, and the ironical fact is that now he has something to complain about, there seems nobody specifically to complain to. So his regular epistles, in barely decipherable hand, go unresponsively to rest with the buffer-stop of the office manager.

If there isn't a handy half-commission man to whom, on an inspiration, Mr. Losingsore may be thought to belong, his strictures are secreted aside for future attention.

This is not half the fun it was, of course. Formerly, one could be sure of prompting some response, however terse, on which to draw for further inspiration. Now, he is compelled to relent, pitifully, . . . "but I realize my business is very small," and wonders why courtesy admits of no reply.

Losingsore is one of those clients, incidentally, possessed of an insatiable thirst for knowledge, and inclined to an exactitude that may well necessitate the annual provision of a detailed catalogue of all transactions, irrespective of the fact that contract notes (in duplicate), together with supporting statements of account, have been regularly supplied.

He is a stickler, too, on the matter of punctuality. Timing, admittedly, is often the essence of the contract in investment, but before breakfast or late at night, dragged towel-swathed from the bath, Losingsore considers his broker's time unreservedly at his disposal. He will positively insist, for example, on the provision of a laboriously collected list of prices by noon sharp, but admit of no reciprocal obligation to be within a mile of the telephone at the appointed hour.

Returning in the late afternoon after a prolonged luncheon, he is surprised to find his broker absent over a hastily snatched sandwich.

Occasionally Losingsore attempts, in desperation, to run his quarry to ground at their place of business, but everybody always seems to be unremittingly "Out" on the office situation board.

"Sorry, sir," evades the resplendent messenger, "Lord Goring's lunching round at the Bank." The telephonist confirms that Mr. Pluckett's just "popped out", while others on the letter-heading seem variously unavailable.

Mr. Losingsore protests, suspiciously, but didn't he catch a glimpse of young Punt's back-view disappearing into a doorway down the passage? "Ah!" The messenger is suitably enigmatic. "I said he was engaged, sir. Might the Head Statistician help you?"

Resurrected from beneath a welter of paperwork, the Head Statistician who is the ultimate arbiter when all other avenues are exhausted, patiently reverses a purchase of 75 *General and Engineering Industries,* when Losingsore had meant 175 *General Engineering (Radcliffe),* supplies half-a-dozen statistical cards on suspended plantation companies, plus a plastic beaker of office tea, and returns to an institutional investment scheme for the deployment of £500,000.

Leaving the office, his coat pockets abundantly sprouting financial literature, Losingsore reflects that these people seem very busy these days.

# Banco on Kropperlabongo

We're all share-smitten in Cedar Grove these days. It's happened since young Trickett bought The Grange, with a 30-foot frontage and a 99 p.c. mortgage. Now, having secured personal bank loans for re-styling our kitchens, we're able at last to indulge a long-cherished ambition to play the stock market.

Trickett, who dignifies himself a "stockbroker" on the strength of his role as an order clerk in a broker's dealing box, is our unfailing mentor and guide to the mysteries of the Square Mile. Attired in charcoal-grey, as a slight concession to the commercial sobriety of his scene, but conceding less in the matter of hair-style (reminiscent of the working end of an industrial mop), he attends regularly of an evening in the saloon of our local, the Leather Bottle.

There, where we used to wax endlessly eloquent over the following Saturday's League games, all our talk now is of price-earnings multiples, yields, growth, cash flow, and a great deal more of which we have only the sketchiest of knowledge.

In fact, young Trickett's formula for successful investment owes surprisingly little to the inhibiting restraint of prosaic facts and figures; instead, he gives refreshing speciousness to financial opinion by ardently following the meteoric stars of the investment firmament.

His ear is attentive, it seems, to many obliging horses' mouths, and he chats cosily about the big entrepreneurs of the corporate world with the familiarity of a close confident.

Anything with the lost savour of rampant tropical growth and present financial decay, rumoured for resurrection on the strength of a couple of Nissen huts in Stepney, then Trickett's on to it with unbounded enthusiasm.

"Dickie Wobble's buying," he would confide in an awed whisper, looking mysteriously around. "He's already got a 10 p.c. stake. Going to make it go with a bang. What's the price? – 13p to 14p, a penny out either way in fifty thou. But, look here, promise you won't buy many. Interfere with the market, and the deal could be off."

And we'd all passionately protest our discretion to the grave, and then make various excuses to get to the phone. To Trickett's credit, what with Bukit-this and Bantam-that, getting nimbly in and out of a succession of potential "shell" operations, to the harassment of our respective stockbrokers, we all did very nicely for a time.

Then one day old Joe, our jovial landlord, who gave a quizzical half-ear to our investment deliberations, respectfully opined that *Belchers*, his brewery, might stand the chance of a takeover bid. He had built up a nice little parcel of the ordinary over the years, it transpired, and had frequently met the chairman, Colonel Belcher at licensed victuallers' dinners.

But Trickett quickly shot that one down – in flames. "Not an earthly," he pronounced authoritatively. "No, no, much too big for anyone to handle. You want to go for the small fry up north. Take *Slopshire Ales*, now, I hear Albie Fizzlestein's been buying his way in for some time."

A fortnight later, when Trickett was conveniently absent with a chill, *Belchers* received a bid from the ever-covetous *Plastic Caterers*, which hoisted its shares a massive fifty per cent overnight.

Which was unfortunate as the rest of us had all gone banco on *Kropperlabongo Rubber*, whose quotation was promptly withdrawn by the Stock Exchange Council.

Now we are all having to do-it-ourselves in the matter of kitchen alterations, which is really a saving, as I attempted to explain to my wife, since it keeps us out of the, as it is now re-named, Plastic Bottle of an evening.

# New Brooms

It was the staff's annual dinner. Jimmy Tipluck, the firm's newly appointed ideas man, sat dejectedly at the festive board, an exploratory fork poised over his portion of Christmas pudding. His thoughts were far away. He was feverishly racking his brains for a last gleam of inspiration.

Across the table he caught the senior partner's eye, and summoned a sickly smile. The other responded with a heavily confidential wink. Which was the more confusing to the care-stricken Tipluck, who was already past the eleventh hour for his promised first revelation, and had not yet set a coherent thought on paper.

Indeed, Jimmy had been increasingly surprised over pre-dinner drinks at his boss's evident benevolence, particularly when he had been slapped on the shoulder with a whispered entreaty for another "cracking good selection".

Jimmy had joined stockbrokers Messrs. Kilcroak, Hengle, Finglestein only a few weeks before Christmas in response to their advertisement for an Original Researcher. It had not been the firm's year, not with the ardent advocacy of Handley Page in January and the impassioned strictures about the folly of Australian nickel speculation just before the first Poseidon strike. It was felt that the humble stats department, diligently ploughing the portfolio furrow, needed the spice of expertise, the spur of the academic analyst.

So the oracle came amid acclaim and relief, not least by the staff whose seasonal bonus hung precariously in the balance. The higher echelon breathed afresh. Even at this late hour, it was felt, there was still the hope of snatching the commission account from the brink of the red.

The most junior partner, delegated the responsibility of working an accommodation miracle, cast around desperately for somewhere suitably befitting the status of the master mind. "Well, what about the little cubicle the lady cleaner keeps her brushes in?" he finally came up with. "You know, next to the loo, where the two attaches sit?"

"H'm, we don't want to offend the cleaner," pondered the office manager. "Still, I suppose we could squeeze him in there – built-in desks, filing cabinets, and so on."

With improvisation, the two attaches banished, the lady cleaner's materials removed, despite protest, up the outer office chimney (in a cupboard, as the builder assured, nicely contrived in the space available). Tipluck was finally put to work with a prodigious amount of stationery. At least, that was the assumption from the rapt silence behind his door.

The younger partners nodded sagely, assured something big was cooking. The senior partner, who had a preference for his nose in investment matters, became given to asking rather testily at intervals: "What's that fellow doin', d'you think?"

After a week, during which Tipluck emerged from hibernation only once, to request the services of a personal secretary, and the lady cleaner was observed to pop in on him occasionally, perhaps from force of habit, but once carrying two plastic beakers of tea from the hot drinks vendor, impatience got the upper hand of curiosity.

"Well, it's agreed, then," said the second senior partner at the next partners' conference, after they had discussed arrangements for the staff Christmas dinner. "We must know what progress Tipluck's making. I'd like to get something out to clients before the holiday." Next morning, accordingly, a small retinue headed by the senior partner, attended by the head stats clerk and partners various, congested the passage outside the researcher's modest retreat.

Tipluck had been duly warned of the visitation. The fruits of his unremitting, but totally abortive, labour were impressively displayed on the working top down one side of the cubicle – a series of charts, meticulously done with their zigzag progressions in red, blue, and green, piles of closely written notes and calculations; sheaves of typewritten material.

"Come, now," said the senior partner, stepping forward with bristling efficiency, "let's see how far you've got." His newest employee gulped. "Well, sir, it's a research in depth, you see. It takes time to assemble the findings. Look here, and here again. . . ." He gesticulated hopefully about the charts. Then throwing caution to the winds, decided to play it by ear, and talked volubly of plunging necklines, double bottoms, and triangles.

"So, you see," he ended up at a gallop, "this approach thus obviously aims at the achievement of sound information and statistical analysis brought to fruition by the application of correct timing." He paused for breath, and glanced apprehensively at the row of faces looming in front of him. They registered everything from the blank to the frankly disbelieving.

The senior partner, who knew not a thing about chartist lore, felt that his youngest partner, but newly returned from a course on Stock Exchange practice, probably did. He jumped in at the deep end. "Excellent!" he proclaimed, in a tone of decision. "A most lucid appraisal of the situation. What d'you think, Hengle?"

*He crept furtively down the passage and slipped into the tiny office*

The second senior partner, who felt he had perhaps inadvertently missed the point, thought it prudent to concur. And the youngest partner, momentarily distracted by the curves of one of the mini-skirted typists spied from his point of vantage in the doorway, was dragged back to earth with a bump. "Marvellous, marvellous!" he enthused, and so ecstatically that everyone else joined in a chorus of agreement.

"That's settled then," said the senior partner, briskly, moving to the door. "We can expect your finished circular in a week, at the latest?" But, back in the privacy of his own office, the senior partner felt decidedly ill at ease. Could it really be, he wondered, that his colleagues understood all that mumbo-jumbo? He decided to seek a little private enlightenment.

Watching through a chink in his door until he saw the researcher leave for his lunch, he crept furtively down the passage, and slipped into the tiny office. Adroitly avoiding the cleaner's broom that stood propped against the wall, he approached the desk. Everything seemed as before. But for one small thing. Slap in the middle of the charts, weighed down by a bottle of ink, lay a slip of paper. It was boldly inscribed – in fact there was no mistaking it – *Prospector's Joy 1.30*.

The senior partner gazed blankly at this cryptic message for several seconds before realization burst with a flash. Then he slapped his thigh in huge delight. By Jove! So that's his trump card, is it? Bright fellow. Nothing like keeping ahead. Well, now he'd show the others whether he knew anything about charts! He strolled casually along to the dealing room. "Is there a mining company called Prospector's Joy?" he inquired of the dealer in charge of the Australian arbitrage.

"Yes, sir, a nickel exploration company. A block of shares were introduced here a few weeks ago. They've stuck around twenty-six shillings." "H'm," meditated the senior partner. "Well, anyway, try and pick me up ten thousand. Personal account, you know."

Still oblivious of what had proved for the senior partner in a matter of days his unwitting Midas touch, Tipluck finally struck at his pudding with fatalistic resignation to impending fate. The waiter bent low. "Perhaps we don't care for sweet, sir?" he asked, solicitously.

Across the table, the youngest partner drew his senior's attention to the researcher's delayed attack. "Looks as if he's going for a silver strike," he observed, sarcastically. The senior partner permitted himself some private mirth. "Nickel, I fancy," he corrected. "Nickel."

"Ol' man seems chuffed," observed the lady cleaner, some way down the table. Her neighbour the office messenger, nudged her confidentially. " 'Ad a big go on a mining share, I 'eard. Cleaned up a nice packet."

" 'Ad a good thing meself last week," retorted that good lady, not to be outdone. "Prospector's Joy in the 1.30 at the Pokesbury Park meeting. Come in at a hundred-to-eight, 'e did."

# Losingsore and the Forbidden Fruit

Mr. Losingsore finally retired on Christmas night to a restless couch. What with excess at the festive board in riotous conflict with sundry alcohols, he dreamed disjointedly of prospecting for silver in a giant plum-pudding; pulling with Angles, his stockbroker, a cracker which produced a motto predicting an imminent Stock Exchange coup; and meeting, in a Midlands night club, with a company chairman who let fall prodigious indiscretions in the rosy light of dawn.

From all of which mix-up, it emerged that he was possessed, just for once in his lifetime, with the ultimate gem of information, endowed with the Midas touch. Then, just as the first champagne bottle was about to pop to the congratulations of envious friends, he awakened in a nightmare sweat to the reproachfully wagged finger of a youthful academic from some remote School of Economics.

"Now, now," admonished this spectre at the feast sternly. "No insider-trading, you avaricious parasite. The Stock Exchange Council's just suspended the quotation, didn't you know? All recent bargains cancelled, and a good job too."

After which restless and fruitless night, Losingsore descended to a spartan breakfast to discover, on belated reference to the previous Saturday's paper, that *Celestial Investments*, lately bought on an accountant friend's pious prediction of a rise to eternity, had promptly dropped 15p. Which dejected him still further.

The trouble these days about that contentious investment ingredient "inside information", Losingsore begins to feel, is that it has come to be suspect, under conditions of bids, leaks, and inquests, as much for what it could genuinely be, as for what, ten-to-one, it is not.

Labouring away in the hitherto desolation of his portfolio, he feels himself liable to be the hapless recipient – he who has heard it all before, and invariably lost his shirt – of a prophetic pearl of wisdom ultimately too hot to handle.

"I'm sorry about that one," apologizes his conscientious half-commission man, whose whispered "dead cert" for a takeover has lamentably failed to materialize.

"Don't give it another thought, my dear fellow," his client reassures him, somewhat relieved. "There'd probably have been a Council inquiry. Just get me out if they ever touch the price again, will you?"

Not that his mentor in the market-place is ever conspicuously backward in proffering the forbidden fruit. On the contrary, his youthful ear seems attuned to all the sizzling hot news in Throgmorton Street.

Tapping founts of unbounded knowledge, Angles regularly breathes confidences of priceless potential over the telephone. But it generally emerges, if the founts are more relentlessly tapped, that

*Pulling with Angles, his stockbroker, a cracker . . .*

Angles's wife's cousin believes it to be true, or that the sub-manager round at one of the bank's suburban branches thought he overheard it from the Securities Clerk.

"But do you know for certain?" Losingsore presses.

Angles hesitates. "Well, I wouldn't like to say, for certain. Fairly certain, anyway."

Which, as Losingsore is rapidly learning from bitter experience, is the fallacy about so-called "inside information". It is more usually half-truth masquerading as fact – an original grain of genuine information so hopelessly tortured by repetition as to miss the mark by a mile by the time it reaches the receptive ear.

As a matter of fact, when it comes to the question of take-overs, bids, special situations, and so on, the signals are usually flown so high and conspicuously, by way of the share price pattern and persistence of buying that the uninitiated have no more than to board the band-wagon with a clear conscience.

The only remaining question then is precisely "When?" Which is quite another matter.

Having deployed his entire capital in a succession of ripe plums, all emitting too much smoke to deny any conflagration, Losingsore, at the end of his patience, finally discards *Miracle Machinery* for the new hope enkindled in *Firework Construction*. But no sooner has he effected the switch than *Miracles* are perversely bid for at 50p over the ruling price, while *Fireworks* after a deceptive splutter subside into oblivion.

As a result, Losingsore's firm resolve is to confine himself to a plain diet and short-dated mortgage debenture stocks in which the sinking fund is attentively present. But I wonder how long he'll keep it up?

# Adrenalin Dries Up on the Up Line

By tacit consent for months past the topic of stocks and shares has been dropped from our conversation in the commuter compartment. Particularly the Colonel, who sold his entire portfolio at the top, has considerably held his former invaluable counsel.

Even a year ago, it was different. Crossing the footbridge to the Up line, we would be impatiently unfurling our newspapers for the City pages, eager to be the first informed about our current fancies, oblivious of fellow-travellers into whom we cannoned.

Breathlessly we would reach our accustomed platform point, wrestling with disarranged sheets of newsprint, and immediately embark on voluble discussion about the previous day's performance. All but the Colonel who had suddenly become interested in farmland.

Nowadays we assemble in chastened mood. Newspapers are discreetly folded. We make what we can of sex, sport, and holiday prospects dimmed in the shadow of our share performance. If the adrenalin is not sufficiently activated by the front page revelation of Dow Jones's further plunge, we take surreptitious peeps into the financial columns to confirm our fears, whilst talking loudly of the fortune of the West Indies. The Colonel contentedly studies the racing form.

The loquacious Jimmy Punt, the half-commission man, alone continues to plough his accustomed furrow, if in unremittingly barren soil. His earlier confidences had not inspired us, or we might have heeded his advocacy of *Army and Navy Stores*. Watching the daily minuses against our luckless selections, we were in no mood for further offerings.

Then just about the time we received our respective brokers' cheques for a wreckage in indiscreet ventures abandoned in final desperation, we learned to our confusion that the Colonel had made some tentative moves back into the market. He was too tactful to tell us himself, but we got the news at secondhand over the domestic grapevine.

When, after a week, the remnants of his Aunt Mildred's little legacy, banked with fervent resolve never again to touch another stock or share, began to burn the inevitable hole in Losingsore's account, his curiosity got the better of discretion. Not that he actually asked the Colonel what he'd bought; just remarked to the compartment at large that Wall Street seemed to be on the mend, and didn't we think it might be time to stake a claim or so in the market?

Stolidly unresponsive behind the rampart of his *Sporting Life* the Oracle declined the bait. But the avid Punt, taking the first cue he had heard for months, jumped in.

"There, that's what I've been telling you," he insisted. "Get in, get in, the water's warm." To which Prickett, who had put a tentative toe in *Primrose Path Developers* only the week before, lamented that he still found it distinctly chilly.

All this furtive angling finally brought an impatient grunt from the Colonel. He emerged from behind his paper with a gesture of submission.

"Stap me, man!" he exploded. "You might come out with it straight. Anyway, I rather gathered you'd all just got out?" he added, with unexpected insight.

"Put ourselves in funds, I'd say," corrected Losingsore, with as much conviction as two inches of bath water. "One must be in a position to take advantage of fresh opportunities, surely?"

The Colonel regarded the compartment with the air of resigned paternalism he might have adopted to his sainted little grandchildren, in the matter of Georgie Best and the greenhouse window – but didn't.

"A most prudent provision," he conceded. "But what you seem to have committed, if you'll forgive me, is one of the cardinal errors of good market timing – you've sold much too late."

We all looked duly crestfallen. Good tactician, the Colonel pushed home his advantage.

"When the investor at large finally reaches the point of slinging out his bits and pieces, it's always, ten-to-one, the time to buy. Talk about redeployment is poppycock. The shares you held will probably rise as quickly on any turnround as any others you might buy. All you're doing is feathering the brokers' nests."

"I thought you said our business was bloody useless to brokers," interrupted Prickett, innocently.

"Yes, yes, I know!" snapped the Colonel. "I was speaking figuratively. Do Malicious Boy for the 3.15 at Pokesbury Park."

Malicious Boy lost.

# The Financial Wizard on the 8.12 to Waterloo

"But there's nothing to go for," laments the Stock Exchange broker, observing the market's repeated attempts to struggle out of the slough. Quotes the jobber, reluctantly venturing his blue pencil to mark still higher a share of which he is obviously short. "But there's no turnover."

Nothing, of course, has perceptibly changed from the day before; U.S. interest rates press unrelentingly higher, another fringe bank flounders, members tip-toe before the lurking spectre of default, markings stagnate on the bread-and-marge line.

Only one thing moves with regularity, if sublime inconsistency. Against all the conceivable odds, the indicator mechanisms recording the hourly changes in the F.T. industrial index, relentlessly click up higher figures.

Mr. Losingsore's broker, Angles, who has harped for months on the virtues of liquidity, is clearly affronted by the perversity of the market. "Keep your powder dry," he had counselled, when he cleared out his client's portfolio. "There'll be wonderful opportunities at the bottom."

Having watched the index climb some 16 p.c. Losingsore is tempted to caustic comment, but on reflection thinks that he had better reserve it for the time when his orders may be on a more defendable basis than a mere 500 shares.

The ever adaptable Angles is converted, meantime, to the view that the market may have "turned". As he now points out, with abundant truth, you can never hit the absolute bottom. Losingsore is promptly the recipient of several bought Contract Notes on the well-tried principle that one should deploy a proportion of one's cash on the first consolidated rise.

At which point, young Algy Losingsore, nurtured on a hardly sustaining diet of *B.L.M.* and *Triumph Investment*, takes to nipping down early of a morning to secrete the paper, so sensitive is the parental attitude to the plusses and minuses in the share columns. Domestic serenity preserved, his parent is compelled to contain his curiosity until reaching the station, while cursing the inefficiency of the newsagent.

The sagacious Colonel, financial wizard of the 8.12, at once divines the truth about all this inconsequential by-play when Losingsore closes their compartment door with a surprising excess of energy for such a tender hour of the day.

"Ah, back in the market, I see," he observes, dryly.

And from the embarrassed rustlings of closely confined readers, not to mention ashen faces raised questioningly after perusal of the C.B.I.'s latest industrial survey, it seems as if more than one has committed his cherished wherewithal for the next Settlement.

As the Colonel is then prompted to explain, the invariable difficulty with the Stock Exchange, in getting out of a trough, is that everybody looks for positively good news, and disappointingly fails to find any.

"It's a truth of human nature," he adds, "that most people greatly distrust what they cannot logically explain. Most offensive these days, particularly, when the young are schooled in adoration of computerized formulae."

"But look at what the chartists say," wails young Jimmy Punt, the half-commission man. "They see the index back to 270, most of them."

"Exactly," agrees the Colonel. "So we have the traditional inconsistency of the bloodless boom. Don't forget, the first phase when the market shifts its ground is either for the bad news to be swept under the carpet or for the good to be grossly exaggerated."

"Sounds like a conjuring trick to me," says the perplexed Prickett.

"Not so illusory as it might seem," goes on the Colonel. "It's a contortion of the technical position. What happens on the ground floor is that share values become greatly over-exposed by a massacre in the market-place. Then the chronic stock shortages begin to glare through a perilously thin price structure. Sensing this, would-be sellers hold off. Next, buyers begin nibbling insistently beneath the surface. That's the sequence."

Punt protests, conscious of the deficiencies of his own commission account, "But still there's no business?"

"That's historically true of pivoting points," explains the Colonel. "The market has to jack itself up by the old 'boot straps' routine until a two-way trading basis is reached. Directly tired holders are able to extricate themselves by a sufficient mark-up, they are seduced yet again. Up or down, the market is self-creative."

Nobody is wholly convinced, except the Colonel himself who composes for slumber until forcefully awakened by impact with the buffers at Waterloo.

# Nothing so Crude as a Tip

"There's nothing nowadays so crude as a tip, Mr. Wakelately," the Hundred-and-Fifth Partner was explaining to the long-absent client. "We long ago gave up making personal judgments or having opinions."

She pertly straightened the jacket of her pin-striped costume, and glanced apprehensively at the deep-tanned man perched on the edge of the chair opposite. He pulled a wry face.

"No, Mr. Wakelately," she insisted. "What happens now is that all your data – age, capital, income, growth requirements, and so on – is programmed; then the Master Computer entirely controls your investment policy. We merely follow instructions – buy or sell."

" 'Wasn't like that when I was here last," objected the old client. "I seem to remember that everyone had a word for the attentive ear. Carveup, my old half-commer mate, used to sink the beers with me in Slaters, where the boys dropped tips like crazy squirrels at nutting time."

His youthful mentor, but lately returned from a course on the Science of Systematized Investment, regarded him with growing disapproval.

"I'm afraid," she said, reprovingly, "you'll find things much changed here since you left for Australia."

"Aw, you make it sound dry as a rusty billy. D'yer mean, no little flutter? Can't I even have a bash at an Aussie nickel now-a'-gin?" he pleaded.

"No, I've told you, private ideas confuse the system," declared the

*The senior partner dismissed the computer with an airy wave of his champagne glass*

Hundred-and-Fifth Partner. She glanced at her watch. "Now, *please*, could we get on. I've a date at 5.30. Are these your record details?" She poised her ballpoint and began methodically to check with him through a four-page questionnaire.

Wakelately answered abstractedly, gazing at the window past which flurries of snow blew gustily down into the narrow, concrete duct between the Stock Exchange and the aggressive modernity of the equally towering office blocks that had sprung up opposite.

The offices all had tiled forecourts and vestibules like vast aquariums, in which to passers-by in the street their occupants seemed to float in an apparently prescribed environment of deep carpeting, plastic walnut veneer, and chromium fittings.

Inside the vast headquarters of Federated Jobbers, the floral arranger could be seen doing the decorations. The jobbers were holding their party that evening for the neighbouring brokers.

Next door, on the twenty-seventh floor of Amalgamated Brokers, the Hundred-and-Fifth Partner hurried through her interrogation, bade her client a breathless farewell, and fled to the powder-room.

It was by then past five o'clock, and the ginwards progression down to the jobbers' party was already crowding the lifts. Halfway to ground level, when the passengers were packed with the intimacy of the metaphorical sardines, a stoutish entrant, achieving the impossible, trod heavily on Wakelately's foot. Recognition instant.

"If it isn't old Carveup! How are yer, mate?"

"Wakey! Well who'd have thought it, after all these years – fifteen, isn't it?"

Considerately transferring his weight elsewhere, Carveup told him that the small firm of stockbrokers, in which he had afterwards been made a partner, had joined Amalgamated as the thirty-ninth in a quickening stream of mergers, and there'd been another couple of dozen since.

"I hunted everywhere for you this afternoon," Wakelately apologized. "Couldn't recognize the place for all the glass and concrete. Ended up with a bossy little grouse-bird on the twenty-seventh."

"Sounds like Miss Pluckworthy," whispered Carveup. "She's got a lot of boy-friends on the 'floor'."

"She's got a lot of sauce. Said I couldn't have a go on my own. I'd have liked a few *Possies*. . . ."

Carveup attempted a warning finger, but was closely confined.

Anyway, his friend was by then so intent on generously imparting his confidences from "down under" that, in the final stampede from the lift, he was past restraint.

"Sssh, no tips!" hissed Carveup. "They're strictly taboo, you know."

Wakelately repented. "Sorry, mate. 'Thought you might like to know what my geologist pal from Kamballie said about the bonanza on the old Lake View property . . . gold, y'know." He shrugged resignedly. "What a miserable bunch you've all become. Anyway, how about a celebration beer? We'll slip round to Slaters? Well, Lyons, then? The Coal Hole?"

But Carveup shook his head.

"They've all gone, Wakey. Office development has killed the lot at the rental values these days. Tell you what, though," he added, "why not join me at the jobbers' party? The whole Street'll be there."

The party, when they got round next door, was already crowding the great dealing room with youthful practitioners. Provocative as was the costume, everybody was decorous and intense. The conversation, from snatches overheard, seemed to centre around the exorbitant cost of modern mechanical techniques.

Carveup explained. "Yes, that's the problem now. Computerization has proved too expensive."

As the tempo quickened, there was a tendency for groups to gravitate into corners, get entrenched behind tables.

At the centre of the most confidentially communicative circle was a young man in a drape suit.

Wakelately plucked at his companion's sleeve. "Tell me, who's the wonder boy?"

"You'd never guess. That, my lad, is our senior partner. Come on, I'll introduce you."

"Well, how are they treating you, Wakelately? Have we done anything yet with your little bit?"

"I'm afraid not," Wakelately admitted. "We're waiting for the computer to come up with something, I understand."

The Senior Partner dismissed the computer with an airy wave of his champagne glass, and for greater stability encircled his client's shoulder to the peril of his canapes.

"Don't you worry 'bout that caper, ol'boy," he said irreverently, then lowered his voice to what he fondly imagined to be a conspirator's whisper. " 'Tell you what, though, you buy yourself a few *Poseidon* – y'know, the ol' Windarra Wonder. Only about thirty pence. Make yourself a crackin' little Christmas box. Gold, y'know . . . they've struck it rich."

Wakelately looked his most innocent. "Good on you, mate," he said. "Right, buy me five thou tomorrow, will you? Well, here's to the computer!"

# Christmas at the Plastic Bottle

Loosestrife is one of those investors who imagine the survival of their shares dependent on unswerving loyalty and patronage. Invest in a supermarket chain, and they'll embark on a pilgrimage to the nearest branch, even at the expense of a gallon of petrol, for no more than a packet of peanuts.

So it was, when limping homeward with a leaky gasket, that he stopped his car in deepest Dorset to consult the "Handbook of Hostelries" enclosed with his certificate for some lately purchased equity in *Belcher's Breweries*.

November dusk was falling, dank and dismal. It was time for the glowing hearth, frothing tankard, twinkling horse brasses, and such other symbols as betoken your friendly tavern.

So with the aid of the interior light, Loosestrife perused his handbook for the nearest accommodation. According to an insert describing newest attractions, this proved to be the Plastic Bottle, at Trumpington Filbert.

Reference to a nearby signpost, which pointed an imperious finger into the night, showed his destination to be two miles distant. Travelling four, he finally circumnavigated the village green across which, into the murk, shone beckoning beams from competing hostelries, but none so penetratingly brilliant as that from the vestibule of the Belcher establishment.

He guessed it was the Plastic Bottle from the lyrical description – the close black-and-white of the timbered gables, the creaking sign, the Olde Worlde charm – all the embellishments the company's designers could bestow.

Inside, sure enough, he could glimpse horse brasses adorning the farthest wall, and the even brassier head of the receptionist. He was received by this lady with such an effusive welcome that he felt it hardly necessary to impress his proprietorship.

Belcher's, for their part, had a more than usually go-ahead management. They prided themselves on cordial relations. In which endeavour they were met on the doorstep by their latest shareholder.

"Now, George, take this gentleman's bag up to number four," she ordered the hall porter. "The best single we've got," she assured Loosestrife.

In a matter of seconds he and his bag were being conducted up the oaken stairway, and along the traditionally ill-lit passage flanked by Morland prints and projecting antiques of angular design. The porter suddenly flung open a door and ushered him into a bedroom.

"Mind the beam, sir," he warned – but too late. "There, you'll have us down. Must be careful y'know."

Loosestrife's forehead had impacted with the blackened lintel of the doorway which gave way comfortably before him. "What the hell!" he exclaimed.

"But didn't you know, sir?" queried the porter. "This is the company's first fibreglass, portable hotel – with plastic attachments, of course," he added. "Erected anywhere in a day; dismantled as quickly. It's the newest thing in catering for events with a passing trade, county shows and the like. Strange you've never heard of us, sir."

Loosestrife felt he had, but having an inherent distaste of all things synthetic, had tried to put it from his mind.

"Not much call in Trumpington Filbert, surely?" he commented.

"Ah, that was for the Pokesbury Steeplechase meeting. Brings down a big crowd does the Pokesbury."

Resigned to a night of plastic simplicity, Loosestrife submitted himself to soft lights, red paper napery, the insistent whisper of taped music, and a bill next morning less digestible even than the breakfast with which it was presented.

Three weeks later the post contained an impressive envelope emblazoned with the Belcher arms. Thinking it some official communication, Loosestrife tore it open and scanned the contents. Next instant, with attempted sleight of hand, he secreted the letter beneath a seed catalogue. It was only the proximity of a coffee cup that impaired his dexterity.

"What's that, Henry?" asked his wife in the mechanical tone intuitive women are apt to use from behind the screen of a newspaper.

"Oh, nothing, dear," evaded her husband.

"Not one of your investments gone down the drain?" pressed Mrs. Loosestrife, adroitly removing her husband's post to insert a plate beneath the spreading coffee stain.

Firmly in possession of the post, Mrs. Loosestrife retired to satisfy her curiosity behind the bulwark of her coffee service. As she read the brewer's letter, her expression changed from mystification to delight.

"But how delightful, Henry!" she exclaimed. "The whole Christmas weekend at the Plastic Bottle, for two, it says. You never told me you'd been the thousandth guest?"

"But I didn't know until now," groaned her husband, who had made plans for a quiet break at home divided between urgent chores and resuscitation at the local.

"Of course we'll accept," said his wife, in a tone of decision. "Now, what shall I wear? Colonel Belcher's the chairman, isn't he? Will his wife be there?"

Loosestrife rose from the table with an air of resignation.

"I really couldn't say, dear. I merely hold a hundred shares."

"Well, you'll not forget to send an acceptance?"

Irritably Loosestrife seized the post from his wife's plate and stuffed it into his pocket.

"No, dear," he spluttered, gulping down a mouthful of toast. It was only later that he found all he had pocketed was the seed catalogue.

On the Friday before Christmas, Loosestrife absented himself early from work intent on getting away ahead of the westbound traffic. At 5.30, they were ensnarled at Wincanton; by 6.15, part of a blasphemous procession in the vicinity of Sherborne.

They finally reached Trumpington Filbert exhausted, hungry, and past dinner-time. Loosestrife swept with a screech of brakes – and profound relief – round the village green – and stopped. There to the convenience of the traveller stood, as in bygone times, the Blue Boar, the Chequers, the Plume of Feathers. And there, too, between two rows of charming cottages, a yawning gap of rubble-strewn ground.

"Well?" queried Mrs. Loosestrife, in that accusative tone women adopt when they've a great deal to say, and assuredly, in the fullness of time, intend to say it.

What her husband should have asked, in a placid way, was. "But didn't you have the invitation, my dear?" In fact, his observance owed less to the season's claims to goodwill than he could later have wished, with the result that a rustic in the porch of the Blue Boar spilt half his jar of cider.

"You took the post," his wife pointed out, searching fruitlessly in her handbag.

"I took the seed catalogue," corrected Loosestrife. "I merely wrote the acceptance. But don't you see, woman," he exploded, "the blasted Plastic Bottle could be absolutely anywhere now from Land's End to John O'Groats."

They put up for the night at a competitor's motel, where the manager, despite the hour, obliged with some pressed beef sandwiches.

**DONALD COBBETT**

It's now half a century since Cobbett - 'The Scribe', as they jocularly called him - first strayed, in the days of the Great Slump, to the ever intriguing Street called Throgmorton. "... a writer who has spent a lifetime among the tycoons and ticker tapes..." was how the later London Evening News introduced his week's run of short stories, entitled the 'Money Maze', in October, '68.

He has spent over forty years on the 'floor' of The Stock Exchange, graduating from humble Blue Button clerk to broker-member and has been a financial columnist for most of this time. Twelve years for the erstwhile *Statist*, three for the *Stock Exchange Gazette* and six for *Business and Finance*, the Irish Republic's leading financial journal. In addition being responsible for the series featuring the lamentable invester 'Mr. Losingsore' in the *Sunday Telegraph*. Using many pseudonyms - 'Veritas', 'Marketeer', 'Donald Buckley', 'Nicholas Lane', 'Sigismund', he has written many special articles and instructive series on investment practice ...pure fiction even, for the financial Press. Ever versatile, his contributions have ranged almost impertinently from *The Banker* to *Honey*, from *Accountancy* to *Annabel*. And withal, he has found time to talk about investing, on the radio occasionally, and speaking officially for The Stock Exchange over many years. He was on the lecturing panels of both The Institute of Bankers and Associated Speakers.